SAVANNAH DOGS III

SAVANNAH DOGS III

MINNIE MCQUILLEN BEIL
EDITOR

FREDERIC C. BEIL

SAVANNAH

TO

OUR AGENCIES

Humane Society of Chatham–Savannah
Pet Assistance League of Savannah
Save-A-Life Animal Welfare Agency
Second Chance Dog Rescue and Referral

AND OUR
DOCTORS OF VETERINARIAN MEDICINE

Amy Ahles
Debbie Barrett
Melanie Bevere
Richard W. Bink
Patrick Bremer
Daniel Brogdon
Al Camacho
Jerry L. Case
Kyle Christiansen
Ernest Compton
Max M. Cooper
Marnie Dasher
DeAnna Douglas
James E. Ducey
Pamela Fandrich
Christopher Gall
Heather Gill
Alan C. Gross
Julie Harelson
Stephanie Hazlett
Don H. Howard
David Howes
G. Scott Hudspeth
J. Patrick Hudspeth

Karen Kane
David B. Kicklighter
Sarah Klunk
J. Stanley Lester
Deana Livingston
Carla Case McCorvey
Lesley Y. Mailler
Steven M. Marlay
Beth Martin
Peter Winn Martin
Chad Nance
Rachel Peeples
Robert Pernell
Cathy Rowan
Billy C. Sanders
John D. Schoettle
Paul Shealy
Michal Soosar
Terri Sparks
Tricia Starnes
Charra Sweeney-Reeves
Brandt Tolbert
Michele Trammell
Donald R. Webb
Allison K. Witherow

Every creature is full of God
and is a book about God.

—Meister Eckhart

CONTENTS

CONTENTS

CONTENTS

CONTENTS

EDITOR'S NOTE

I find it hard to believe that it has been three years since we published the inaugural edition of *Savannah Dogs*. That would be twenty-one dog years. And now here we are with our third edition, *Savannah Dogs III*. Similar to our first two volumes, you will find page after page of stories about dogs who make their homes in Savannah.

I have never tired from meeting new dogs and asking them to tell us their stories. In the parks, at flea dips, just walking downtown, I met most of the dogs you will be introduced to in these pages. I know that you will find these canine tales just as fascinating as I did.

Thanks to the many dogs and their packs who contributed to this third edition. Again, all royalties resulting from the sales of this book will be contributed to four Savannah agencies that support our dog community.

As always, on behalf of my entire species I extend our collective gratitude to those precious humans who rescue and adopt us and welcome us so warmly into their packs; to all the veterinarians who care for our health needs; and to all who protect our well-being.

Our stories are a testimony to how much we are loved. Thank you.

MINNIE MCQUILLEN BEIL

The first time I met John was at the Humane Society. I'd been wandering the streets for the first six months of my life. I'm not sure what happened to my mom or my dad. Most of that time is a blur anyway.

So there I am, scared as hell with no idea what would happen next. In walks John, and he's moving up and down the hall checking out all the detainees. He stops at my cage and, breaking every rule, opens the door and reaches for me. Not knowing who he was, I backed into a corner of my cell, trying to get away from him. I'm not a biter, so I let him pick me up. He's got me under the armpits, a stupid grin plastered across his face, and I just stare back at him. He puts me under his arm and walks me outside. Freed at last, I amble off and "take care of business," all the time looking over my shoulder trying to figure this guy out. He looks pretty harmless, not like some of the schmucks I'd met on the street. So I figure, what the hey, I've got nowhere else to go. I walk toward him, sit between his feet, look up, and give him the big doe-eyes treatment. He was putty in my paw. Mama, I'm going home!

Come to find out he's in the food business and the chow from day one was the stuff of dreams! Liver pâté, smoked salmon, lamb chops, beef tenderloin—no complaints from me. Sure I get the canned-and-dry dog "food" every morning, but come nighttime, I'm treated to some damned good grub. My heart goes out to my canine brothers and sisters who are forced to eat only those rock-hard pebbles of ground corn meal, basted with "real beef gravy" every day. Okay, enough, I'll step away from the podium.

Anyway, life was pretty good. I lived with John and a chocolate brown little something that he picked up at the Humane Society. Phoebe was my best friend for twelve years, but she had a bad ticker and died three years back. I miss her a lot, but now I've got the house and John to myself.

He's so easy. We've been together for fifteen years and, honestly, I could have done a lot worse. Phoebe and I used to meet him at the door every night, but with Phoebe gone and my hearing just as gone, he comes to my room and nuzzles and hugs, wakes me up to "go outside," still brings home mucho grande meals, and all he wants in return is a little lick on the nose. I can still do that.

I'll be sixteen in March, and as long as I can, we'll be friends.

DAPHNE

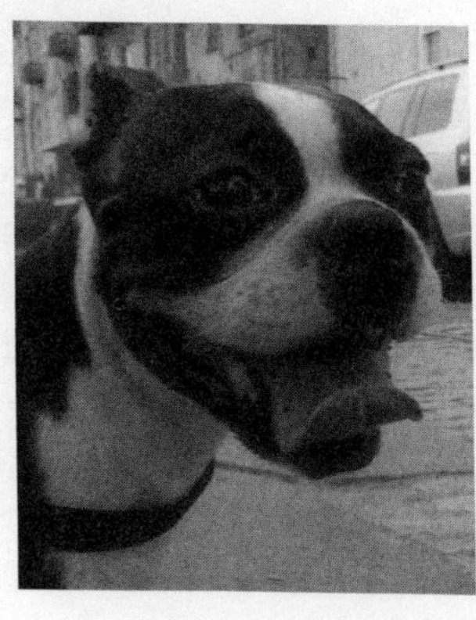

RODNEY KNUCKLES ("RODNEY")

It is an honor to be considered to be a part of such a wonderful book that features all of my new neighbors, who are equally as wonderful. Dante and I have lived in Savannah for just about a month now. We migrated south from Kent, Ohio.

Although we left behind many friends and family in the frozen North, we have found Savannah to be a warm and inviting paradise. My owner and I live near Forsyth Park and enjoy strolling through the gardens, chatting with all of my new friends, and making some of the trees my own. I especially like watching the soccer and Frisbee games, though the players will never pass to me for some reason. If they only knew my talents with a Frisbee.

The squares are some of my favorite places to visit during the day. I'm especially fond of Monterey Square, as there are several nice dogs that live nearby and frequent it as much as we do. In particular there are a few very pretty young lady Boston terriers that I have had my eyes on from time to time. I really consider myself lucky to live in the neighborhood that I do. My building has four other dogs living in it. And like I said,

I will never get tired of gossiping in the park with all the other canines.

When I am "good," Dante takes me down to River Street for some of the parties and festivals, where I get to meet people from all over the country. Last weekend I even watched some fireworks at night. The walk to River Street is a lot more fun though. It's so nice how the shop owners will put out bowls and buckets of water for all of us to drink from. It can get really hot down here, I have noticed; and remember, I don't have the luxury of taking off my fur coat, or for that matter even getting a summer haircut. I like to take a break right around Chippewa Square and relax in the shade for a few seconds; sometimes I even do my best Forest impression for the passing tourists. It's good, but it needs work.

My friend Jack the Weiner (dachshund) asked me the other day, "Rodney, what is your favorite part about Savannah so far?" And I told him, "Jack, I'd have to say the children that love to pet me and give me kisses. They make me feel young again, as I am turning three (human years) in September. I then told him, "Another thing that I love about it here is that unlike Ohio, where it was cold and I had to stay inside for almost half of the year, down here I am able to cruise around town all year long."

Dante and I love the city so far, but we love the people here even more. Thank you, to all of our new- found friends.

RODNEY

4

WOOF

One day, four years ago, Woof, named by our granddaughter who called all dogs "Woof," became a member of our household. How he came to join us is a tale of conspiracy.

Ed had been reluctant to set aside his mourning clothes that he had donned two years earlier on the death of Woof's predecessor. Galumpus, a half-Catahoula, half-Lab male, had been devoted to us for eleven years. His sole purpose was to please us.

We became convinced that a conspiracy between our friends Bob and Eileen and their friends Bill and Rhonda was conceived to overcome our reluctance to consider another dog. Bob and Eileen invited us as well as Bill and Rhonda to a crab boil. We talked about the crabs—big, plump, blue crabs trapped in Bay St. Louis by Bob. We talked of how Bob had cooked and seasoned the crabs; they were wonderfully cooked and seasoned. We talked about the weather. It had been a beautiful, clear day, and now the sun was just setting. Then Ed and I became aware that the conversation had turned to dogs. Since Bob and Eileen were our neighbors, they knew of Galumpus. We were surprised that

Bill and Rhonda knew of him, too. Obviously Bob had talked to them about Galumpus.

Rhonda then began to tell a story of how she had acquired a puppy that she felt unable to keep, for she already had two dogs.

Here is her story. One afternoon, while dropping off a friend at an apartment, she heard a male scream, "I told you not to get a g...... dog." Rhonda saw the man kick the puppy, which went flying. She also saw a crying baby on a picnic blanket. She assumed the puppy had playfully nipped the baby. That must have angered the father. He scooped up the baby, as well as the picnic basket and blanket, leaving his wife and puppy to follow. The puppy sat in confusion. Rhonda thought that if the puppy followed, he would be an abused member of that family. If he wandered off and crossed the street, he would be killed. Neither option was acceptable to Rhonda. So she scooped up the puppy ("kidnapped him," in her words) and took him home. Again there seemed two options: either take him to the SPCA or find him a home.

When Bill told the story to his coworker Bob, that was when—Ed and I believe—the conspiracy was born. Bob probably thought of the idea of having a crab boil—he knows that Ed and I love broiled crabs—to give Rhonda a chance to tell her story to us.

Ed and I were sufficiently impressed with Rhonda's story to share her hope that a home might be found for the puppy. Ed even thought that he might be ready to put aside his mourning clothes for the "right dog." However, we knew nothing of the puppy except what Rhonda could tell us—that is, that it was a fluffy, black puppy of apparently gentle disposition. Ed suggested that perhaps I could drive the sixty miles to evaluate the puppy. But the next morning a cell-phone call from Bill announced that he was on his way to our house with the puppy.

What dog lover can resist a fluffy, affectionate, sweet-breath puppy?

So Woof joined our family. He grew to be a beautiful, fifty-pound, black, long-coated, child-loving dog. Although he is of indeterminable ancestry (our veterinarian said that if there were such a thing as a black Irish setter, we had one), whatever his heritage, we and our grandchildren are delighted to have him as part of our family.

EDWARD ROGGE AND DEE ROGGE

U-CDX Southchase's Georgia Rebel
CD, NAP, NJP, TDIA
("Rebel")

I'm a black-and-tan coonhound. I was born nearby at the very prestigious Southchase Kennels under the watchful eyes of Lynda Webb and Stan Bielowicz. My mom (Cynthia Lord) brought me home to Savannah to live when I was very young.

I was soon introduced to a trainer named Carol Mett. She convinced my mom to enter me in obedience trials. What was she thinking! A hound at an obedience trial with all those retrievers and border collies! After all, every hound knows that "the nose rules." But in spite of this I was able to eventually acquire three obedience titles.

I was also introduced to another trainer, Karen Corio. After much encouraging and training, my mom decided to enter me in agility trials. After many trips, I finally acquired two agility titles.

This was all very stressful to my mom. I think she needs to learn to relax, have fun, and be creative. I really excel at being creative in the ring. People always enjoy watching me at obedience and agility trials just to see what new move I can create. One of my most famous is the pause at the top of the A-frame to sit and pose for my photo moment. I've also been known to walk up to a high jump and then jump over it as opposed to running up to it and jumping over it in one fluid movement. Another time I decided to step over the first board of the broad jump and then go over the other three instead of jumping over all four at the same time.

Of course what I do best is to follow my nose. After all, that is what I was bred to do. My mom and I live on the marsh, and I do so enjoy hunting down all the little varmints that come into the yard.

Another thing I enjoy tracking down is friends. I have made lots friends at all the trials my mom has taken me to. I also have two really good Scottish friends (the terrier kind) named Ceilidh and Faeden and their mom, Ginger Robertson, who I travel with. (A third Scottie named Seumas also used to travel with us, but sadly he recently passed away and will now travel with us in spirit only.) The best part about going to trials is being with my friends and staying in motel rooms with really comfortable beds.

As a certified therapy dog, I have also made lots of friends at the nursing homes I visit. The residents seem to enjoy seeing me and petting my lovely black-and-tan self. One day they even surprised me with some garlic and peanut butter treats made especially for me. I really liked that! One of my best friends at the nursing homes was Mr. Brown, who used to regale me with tales of his coon-hunting days (or nights rather) and had lots of advise on how to deal with the pesky critters. Sadly, though, he has passed, but I know that I'll see him again one day at the big hunting lodge in the sky.

For several years I have also made friends at the summer event held at the Savannah Mall, which is sponsored by the Savannah Kennel Club. I enjoy meeting all the people and welcome all the attention. My mom thinks I am the epitome of good nature. I guess that's why I make friends so easily.

I only wish that I had a better friend to live with. I have to stay with a really pushy bloodhound named Daisy. She thinks everything belongs to her. She never lets me sit on any of the furniture or in the swing out in the yard by the marsh that I especially like. She's a very sloppy eater as well and is always dropping pieces of food, but I dare not pick any of it up. She also thinks she is supposed to go out the back door first. As I said, she is very pushy, bossy, and overbearing. But I guess we all have a cross to bear.

Meanwhile, I'll just keep going places with my mom and making more friends (of the doggy and human kind). Maybe I'll even earn another title someday. If not, maybe I can teach my mom to relax and smell the roses (or dog treats, rather).

REBEL

10

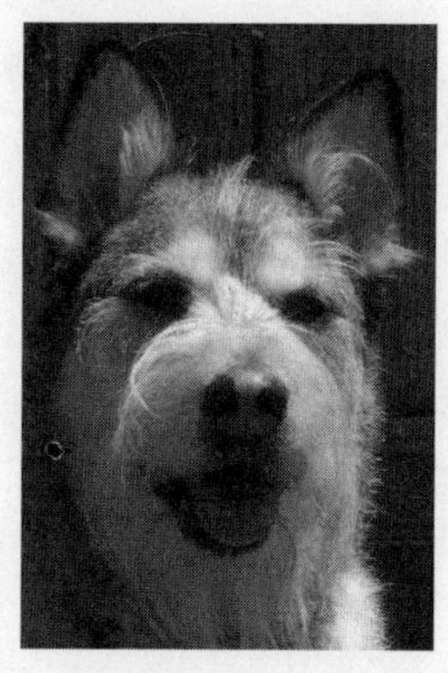

Lara Croft Kirk
("La La Girl")

I had a really hard time as a puppy. I was found in the middle of the road when I wasn't even a year old. Although the family that found me was very nice to me, they had other dogs I couldn't get along with. They brought me to the Humane Society in the hope that I would find a good home.

I was kept there for a week to make sure I was healthy enough to be adopted out. I will never forget the first day out. I saw a couple looking at me, smiling, and then telling me how cute I was. I started to bark because I knew that was my family. I was adopted my first day out.

During my first couple of months with my family, they found out that I was afraid of a kind of affection. I was scared of people, kids, and dogs. I couldn't walk past manholes or gutters. I was a frightened dog with no confidence.

One year later I started to feel safe. I allowed them to hug me and show me affection. My owners took me on long walks on River Street and had me socialize at PetSmart. People would tell me how cute I was and how I needed to be in the movies. That really boosted my ego. Soon my fear of walking past gutters and manholes passed. I still didn't like children and other dogs. My owner called a pet psychic to help her to understand me better and to work with my issues. She found out some disturbing things that had happened to me, which brought tears to my owner's eyes. My original owners were very cruel to me during my puppy hood. Everything that the psychic said shined some light on why I acted the way I did. I am still working through my problems.

My mom worries about my seizures and thyroid problems that developed a year and half ago. It is consent trips to the vet. I am not thrilled either. I hate needles. Even though I have these problems, my owners have worked with me every step of the way. I have been to PetSmart for advance training classes and clicker training. I learned lots of tricks and in the process have learned more, too. I also go to agility classes, where I jump and also walk the balance beam. My parents have taken me on vacations, too.

We've been to the mountains, where I hiked and swam, and to Florida, where I walked on the beach. I am looking forward to the trip we are taking to Illinois soon. I would like to see the Sears Tower. My mom also takes lots of pictures of me and then sends them to animal agencies. Mom and other people think I belong in the movies.

I am four years old now and still working on my issues. I am, however, very happy and have a lot more confidence. My owners have loved me through thick and thin. I know that with love and guidance from my owners I will be the best dog I can be.

I hope that I will see you at the movies.

LA LA GIRL

DIXIE

This is the story of how a very special dog came into our lives. My wife and I lived in Wichita, Kansas, at the time, and the story starts on a day that changed so many lives—September 11, 2001.

We had plans to fly to Florida for vacation to meet at Disney World with my sister and her family from the UK. Our travel date was September 12, 2001. Well, as we all know too well, nobody traveled anywhere by air on that day. Our big vacation was cancelled, so we took a road trip for a short break. On the day after our return, still feeling very down about what had happened, my wife suggested we visit the Sedgwick County animal shelter. So on September 18, 2001, we walked into the shelter and started looking at all the dogs and cats. We walked past a small black-brown-and-white dog sitting very quietly in her cage. The dog's eyes met ours; she had huge brown eyes. We both stopped and looked at each other. And smiled. We turned round to look at this little puppy again. Together we nodded. This dog was for us. We went to the desk and asked about the little black, brown, and white dog. The staff told us that she was about six months old and that she had been abandoned at the shelter on the morning of September 11, 2001. Actually, she had been dumped at the front of the shelter before the employees had even arrived to work that day. We asked if we could adopt her and they said yes. After filling in the paperwork and handing over a few dollars, she was ours.

We named her Dixie, because it just seemed to fit her. After we brought her home, she became the best friend and playmate of our other dogs. She soon showed how smart she was, and gave away some idea of her heritage. She tries to herd the other dogs. We think she is part Border collie, part beagle, and part spaniel. As she grew, her coat changed from short to long and flowing.

When a change of job brought us to Savannah, Dixie came with us of course. Dixie spends most days sleeping on the couch with occasional visits to the backyard to chase squirrels and birds. Dixie has a brother Max, a terrier mix; brother Bosco, a Chihuahua mix who is her best buddy; and a sister Emma, an Aussie cattle-dog mix. Dixie certainly cheered us up during those dark days in September 2001 and has been the light of our lives ever since.

DIXIE'S DADDY

BO JANGLES NEWMAN ("BO")

Hello there! I am a golden retriever. I was born on Thanksgiving Day 1992. I can still smell all that good food. To this day I love fresh vegetables and fruit.

When I left my mother, I did not go to live with the family I live with now. I lived next door to them. They had a dog named Chance. He and I became best friends. Sometimes I would go over to visit, and Chance and I would run and play. Sometimes we would just run up and down the fence in our respective yards.

Then one day, when I was about nine months old, my owner gave me to Amanda and her mom, Mary. I have been with them ever since. I have had a really good life, lots of love and care, and also a really great best friend.

When I was about one and a half years old, I had my first seizure. It really scared me and my family. I accidentally bit Mary's hand, and she had to go to the hospital. But with her care and love and my veterinarians, Dr. Sanders and Dr. Fandrich, I have had only a few seizures in all these years.

A couple of years ago a new dog moved into our house. A little girl named Norma Jean. I think she thinks that I am her dad or brother. She sticks to me like glue.

If I sleep, she is right there practically laying on top of me. She follows me around the house and the yard. Outside she runs circles around me and bites at my heels until I play with her. Even though I am older, I can still play and have the best time like I am two years old again. My favorite game is rolling back and forth in my favorite spot in the yard, scratching my back and barking.

I live with cats too. There are three of them: Hailey, Soot, and Annie. Hailey is older than I am and ill. Soot is black, big, and my friend. Annie is the newest cat, and she does not like dogs at all. I am such a nice guy. If the cats come while I am eating and start eating my food, I let them have it. Mary or Amanda have to come and chase them away so I will finish my food.

Last year I lost my best friend, Chance. He has gone to Dog Heaven. I had a really hard time right after he left. My owners understood how I felt and helped me through it. Chance left me his favorite spot in the house, right in front of the fan. Boy, do I love it.

We just got a new dog; his name is Rok. He used to live behind us, but his owner is leaving for the Army and he gave Rok to us. I live in such a loving home.

I came here when Amanda was in first grade, and she will graduate next year. I really would like to still be here to help her celebrate.

BO

16

Tiffany ("Tiffy Lou," "Ms. Lou," "Prissy Lou")

Our story begins at the 2000 Savannah Dog Show. Wandering in and out of the rows of tents, people, and dogs, I discovered two absolutely adorable puppies. The kind breeder not only introduced them, but let me hold and pet them. They were as sweet as they were adorable, and I fell in love. They were Pekingese puppies, and I had never seen any that were true representatives of the breed. They were so beautiful with their expressive flat little faces. Those babies weren't for sale, so I began a quest to find my very own.

My puppy would be a little girl named Tiffany. My search took me hither and yonder with several leads that didn't work out. Finally, the week before Christmas, I drove to Tallahassee, Florida. The puppy was six months old and the sweetest little ball of fur. She was caramel and cream with white-and-black markings and big black eyes that twinkled. Her tail was a cheerleader's pom-pom across her back. I knew beyond a shadow of a doubt that she was my Tiffany.

When we arrived home she quickly charmed and won the rest of my family—my husband, my cats, and my senior Pomeranian. Tiffany wanted to be friends with everyone.

The Pekingese was once the imperial dog of China. Underneath all that hair beats the heart of a lion, thus the nickname "lion dog." Tiffany has all the traits of her heritage within her person. Now at four years of age, Tiffany is very feminine, regal, and loving. She is also her own unique little person. She barks for her treat, to play, and to go outside. She finds ordinary toys a bore. They must jump, twist, move, and make noise. Her favorite toys are a rabbit on a bungee cord, a red round smiley face that laughs, a dog that barks and says yahoo, and a tiger slinky on an elastic string. During the summer she cools off on the floor vent. She cannot take the heat. The neighbors know her as the dog that loves to visit. If there's an open door, she will invite herself in. Her cousins—Clara (a Boxer), Mr. B (a Shih Tzu), and Wesley (a Yorkie)—know her as the mischievous diplomat that somehow ends up with their treasure. It's all done with a smile and not one cross bark from anyone.

Tiffany's favorite hobby is people-watching, especially when they are working. She finds us very entertaining and could watch us all day. Being curious, she likes to walk in one direction so she can see new things. I usually end up carrying her back. "Walking the dog?" my husband laughs as I return with her in my arms.

Because she is sociable, friendly, loves children, and takes things in stride, I decided to share her with others by joining the other therapy dogs in our city. As the children eye my very furry dust mop, questions begin to roll. Where are her legs? Where are her feet? Why is her nose so flat? Do you color her hair? They love her and she loves them.

Tiffany is my delight and a joy. But beware of all that hair for it does take lots of care!

BETTY RAY

HOPS
("HOPPER")

It was a quiet evening. I'm sure that all four of my cats were silently up to no good while I could hear the faint sound of the television coming from the living room. It was about 9:30 P.M. I had settled into my studio for the rest of the evening. I was ready to work on my graphic freelance. I turned my computer on, and while it was warming up I decided to make some coffee. I was comforted with the idea of a quiet evening, my cup of coffee, and being productive with my freelance. Before I sat down in my studio chair, I raised the blinds in the studio. The two windows looked out into the backyard. The backyard at the time had a small chain linked fence in the back with morning glories twisted along the top. Behind my house is an alley. On the other side of the alley lives a family of five. This family also had a dog. His name was Champ. I used to see the children playing with him in the backyard every now and then. This dog was a golden retriever–cocker spaniel mix. They had gotten the dog as a puppy. I never saw him out of his yard—until that one evening I was getting ready to do my freelance.

As I lifted the blinds and sat down to work, I suddenly

saw the back neighbor's dog trying to get *into* his yard. I thought to myself, that's strange . . . I never see him out. I went to my bedroom to grab my glasses so I could get a better look. I could see that he had his collar on with a leash attached to it. I thought, now that's odd, maybe they were walking him and he got away. I took my glasses off, ran to my bedroom, changed into sweatpants, and headed for the backyard. I unlocked the back gate and called the dog. He immediately came running to me. I proceeded to return him home. I took him to the front door and knocked. The family answered the door. They didn't look very happy that I had returned him. They just said thank you, took the dog, and closed the door. I returned home and called my mother. I told her what had happened. After that I microwaved my coffee for a minute and returned to my freelance, I thought about how I had done a nice thing.

The next day, while doing yard work, my neighbor approached me. She explained to me that it was no mistake that the dog had been on the opposite side of the fence the previous night. She told me that the dog had been dropped off at Daffin Park and had made his way back home. She also said that the dog had one more week before they would drop him off at a park further away so that he would not be able to find his way back home again. It was also mentioned that they might drop him off in traffic so that he would not know which car to follow home. My mouth dropped at the near thought of people treating an animal that way. I offered to keep him in my backyard until I could find him a home.

When I decided to take the dog in, I was determined to find him a home. There were no intentions of keeping him for myself—reason being, I could not have a dog. I was a cat person. I kept the seven-month-old puppy outside. He was not allowed in my house. There was no reason to introduce him to the cats. I wasn't going to keep him.

I did some research and found out that on weekends you could take your pets to PetSmart and possibly get them adopted. This seemed like an excellent idea. I had kept him in the backyard for about a week and figured it was time to get his act cleaned up. I bought him flea medicine, dog food, a leash, two toys, and, oh, a bed. I just wanted to make him comfortable until I found him a family. Plus, I had to make him marketable for the adoption day at PetSmart.

Now it was time to introduce him to the cats. It was just a test. I wanted to see how it would go. There wasn't going to be a tremendous amount of weight put on this one meeting. I just had to get him to the tub. As I let the dog into the house, there was the initial moment of craziness. The dog was excited to be in the house. I took him straight to the tub. The cats were frozen. I gave the dog an oatmeal bath. The bath went amazingly well. After the bath I dried him up and applied his Advantage. Gosh! He smelled so much better. He looked so cute. I could start to feel that feeling of maybe wanting to keep him. I thought, okay, enough of that kind of thinking. Just put him back outside on his beddy with his toy. This coming weekend I would take him to get adopted.

The weekend came. It was time to check out the adoption situation. I packed up all of his stuff. His toys, his bed, his leash, anything he might need for his new family. I started to feel funny packing up all his stuff, but still, I packed it up and threw it all in the car. I started the Jeep. The dog sat in the passenger seat. He was very good in the car. He enjoyed being with me and just driving along. We got to PetSmart, walked in, and as the doors slid open, there were pets everywhere. Some in cages and some on leashes. All standing with their human friend. I went up to one of the PetSmart people and asked how pet adoption worked. She said, "You would come every weekend and sit with your dog while people come up and ask about your dog." I would have to sit there all day with him? I was under the impression that I would just leave him and that *they* would find him the home. It was like a pet garage sale. All of a sudden I looked around, looked at my dog, looked around again, and finally looked at *my* dog, and said, "We're outta here!"

My sister helped me find a new name for him. It was officially Hops. No, we are not beer drinkers; and no, he does not hop. The color of hops, a grain-like barley or wheat, matched the color of his coat perfectly. It's now me, five cats, and Hops. We are all very happy. The last thing I had heard from the family that was planning to dump him was that "he wasn't doing his job" and that was one of the reasons they didn't want him anymore. As far as I'm concerned, he does his job every day. He loves me.

TRISHA ALBANO

TROOPER DAVIS ("SUPER TROOPER")

One day, in February 1991, my husband called me at work at Southside Hospital for Animals. He told me that he had found a puppy near the Rio Gate at Hunter Army Airfield. He said that he had named him Trooper. That night, when I got home, I found a small ball of fluff asleep on Bill's lap. The small fluff was black, with tan on his legs and above his eyes. He also had a voracious appetite. I took him to work with me, and Dr. Karen Kane pronounced him to be in great health. After a short stay at the vet's, he was mine.

That May, Trooper made his first appearance at the Savannah Pet Show and won in his class. Since then he has appeared in thirteen Savannah Pet Shows, winning or placing in his class every year, and even winning a "Best in Show." When Trooper was seven, my friend Kelly Meyer formed Coastal Therapy Dogs. Trooper took the test as a therapy dog and passed with flying colors. Soon Trooper was visiting several nursing homes. He happily spent hours being petted by the residents and starred in a Christmas play at John Wesley Villas.

In 2002 my life went through a dramatic change. My husband and I separated, and I moved to my present home. Trooper helped me through this time, always knowing when I needed a lick or a snuggle. Soon thereafter, because of age and health problems, Trooper retired as a therapy dog. He now spends his days on his couch or patrolling his yard. I now work at Plantation Animal Hospital on Hilton Head Island.

Trooper's health is now in the hands of Curtis Hennessey, DVM, and Mark Doran, DVM, both of whom will do everything possible for Trooper.

Trooper is now thirteen and a half, but he acts like he is five. He's still young at heart and will be lighting up my life for a long time.

DIANE DAVIS

**PARKER
PEPPER
("PARKER")**

How he came to be so neglected is anyone's guess. Maybe a former owner was elderly and could no longer care for him, or maybe he was lost on a vacation expedition. Perhaps he was stolen from a good caring home by people who knew nothing about the care of poodles. But there he was, wandering around Savannah with no collar, home, or sustenance. The limp in his gait was evident, as the eye and ear infections were not.

A young woman named Kelly who lived nearby noticed the dog and its plight and could no longer stand to see the rough-looking creature wander around searching for food and water. As she was having this "conversation" on the curb with this pitiful dog, she told him that she was going to have to take him to the shelter. There was nothing else to do. No one else would touch him. She knew he would be put to sleep and was wrestling with herself on the issue. Suddenly he looked up at her, even though he couldn't see a thing, and wagged his little matted tail. She knew then that he had some life and some spirit left in him. That's when she said, "Get in the car!" Parker must have sensed her kind nature, or was too hungry to back away from help. St.

Francis of Assisi must surely have been watching in approval as Kelly took the dog to Savannah's Pet Complex, where they shaved and bathed the dog, and discovered that he was a standard poodle, and of royal size, at that.

Someone in Parker's past cared enough to take the time to train him in basic obedience, because he was well behaved, calm, and quiet. When Parker was taken to a local veterinarian to get checked out, he had bad ear and eye infections, but no sign of heartworm, so a former owner cared enough about their pet to provide him with heartworm protection and also to have him neutered. We will never know how such a wonderful creature came to such a ruin, but the details of his salvation are clear.

The young rescuer Kelly, a member of PETA, knew that she had to take action. The Pet Complex, being staffed by caring animal lovers, also did not hesitate to help contribute to the dog's salvation. Case Veterinary Clinic, when presented with the sick animal, treated him at cost to the rescuers. And, finally, a new owner, a lover of standard poodles, did not hesitate to take in the orphan and include him in her family of pets.

Parker currently resides in southside Savannah with another standard poodle, a mini-poodle, and a big yard full of agility equipment. He loves to go for rides in the car and gets to run alongside a bicycle on remote county roads at dawn. When it gets hot he gets to travel to Massachusetts for summer vacations; and when it gets cold again, he gets to snuggle in bed with an owner who appreciates just what a fine animal she has been able to incorporate into her life. St. Christopher must be very happy.

ANNE SCHLOTTERBECK

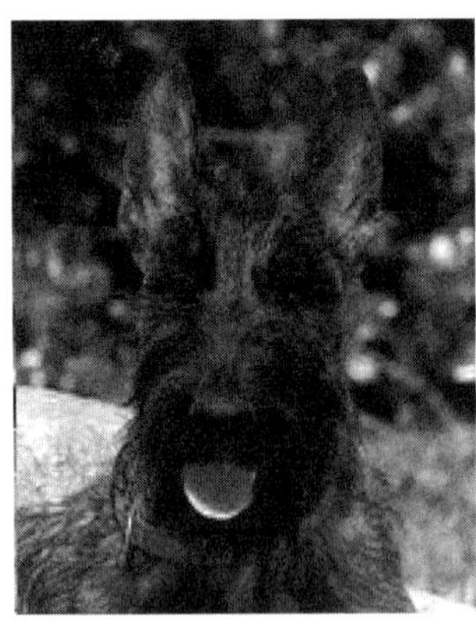

I'm ten months old, and I'm almost full grown. In case you can't tell by my picture, I am a brindled Scotsman. Mom says I have so many highlights in my hair, which looks golden and thus my name, which is Gaelic for golden. My story is just really beginning.

I was born up north—that is, North Carolina. I kenned who my mom was going to be, so when she came to take me home I raced across the room to meet her. Since I wanted to get there first so that I could be sure she would pick me, I left my brother and sisters in the dust. I had a feeling that we were supposed to be together. I just never counted on what was waiting for me at my new home. When we got there, I was met by two more Scotties just like me. One of the Scotties you really would not want to mess with; she is kind of a control freak and thinks she runs the house. The other Scotty is a very nice older gentleman. He no longer lives here. Mom says he has crossed the bridge, but before he left he showed me lots of things—you know, stuff every young lad needs to know, like how to look really really cute when you have done something that you're not supposed to have done. Who would have thought that chewing on a piece of paper would be so bad! But when my dad was yelling, "Where is my check?" I knew I had better start looking really adorable.

My mom says that my real dad is sort of famous; he has lots of letters behind his name and even has had his picture in a magazine and on the cover of a calendar. Mom says if I work real hard I can be just like him. So every week we go to "puppy school" and learn lots of stuff. The most important thing I learned is that at school you get lots and lots of cookies and you do not have to share with anyone. One day I will be old enough to play at all the dog shows we go to, but right now all I get to do is watch. For the time being I guess I'll stay busy keeping the yard free of all those squirrels and lizards. After all, someone has to do it. So I quess I am really like every little boy—I sleep a lot, eat a lot, and want to grow up to be just like my dad.

FAEDEN

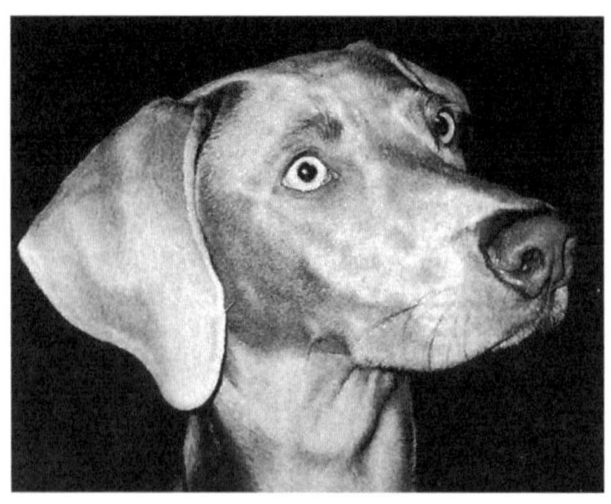

WEISER BLITZ HANNAH
NA, NAJ
("HANNAH")

Meet my ten-and-a-half-year-old Weimaraner. She en-
compasses everything about the breed that I love and that
other people find exasperating. She is stubborn, cunning,
independent, loyal, loving, and definitely the Boss. Add
to this that she has a terrible case of WADD (Wei-
maraner Attention Deficit Disorder), and one can under-
stand that Hannah could have become a problem. But,
on the other hand, she loves children, puppies, and her
people, which includes almost everyone she knows. And
she is crazy about playing ball.

Hannah came to live with us on Christmas Eve 1992.
She was a very lively puppy, and Mom and Dad quickly
decided that obedience training was a must. When she
was six months old, we enrolled her in the first class. The
class lasted six weeks, but Hannah needed more than six
weeks of beginning obedience—heeling on lead, coming
when called, and learning to stay and stand for an exam.
So we reenrolled her in the basic obedience class and then
after that six weeks reenrolled her again. We continued to

take her to the beginner class and even decided to enter Hannah in an obedience match. We started small by entering a class where the dogs compete on lead (leash). Hannah did well, and her obedience instructor and I were so proud that she stood for the exam by the judge without moving. This had been a major obstacle because she didn't like being touched by a stranger.

With this success under our belts, Mom decided that it would be great to get an obedience title. So Hannah and I began to train for the Novice level. Hannah, on the other hand, wasn't thrilled by obedience competition and it showed. Outside of the obedience ring, she would heel next to me with no problem. Inside the ring, she would heel twenty feet behind me. She forgot to sit when we stopped and in general looked completely miserable. After five years and no qualifying scores, she finally convinced me that obedience competition was not her cup of tea.

When she was about eighteen months, we entered Hannah in Conformation competition (beauty contest). The dogs have to run around the ring and let the judge examine them. There are several classes, divided by sex of the dog and age. There isn't always competition in all of the classes, so the opportunity to get the blue ribbon (first place) would seem to be a cinch. Not true. At a show in Charleston, South Carolina, Hannah and I entered the ring, and then were directed to run around the ring so the judge could see how she moved. This was the easy part. The judge, an elderly woman, approached Hannah to examine her. Remember that Hannah didn't like to be "touched" by strangers. She squirmed and bucked and maneuvered so that the judge couldn't touch her. As much as I tried I couldn't keep her from twisting away from the judge. This scenario continued for several minutes before the judge gave up on trying to examine her. Then this woman explained that she couldn't possibly give Hannah a blue ribbon since Hannah refused to be examined by her. So we entered the ring as the only dog in the class and left the ring with a second-place ribbon. Not many dogs can claim that distinction, and I have never seen this done again.

Then Hannah discovered Agility, where she got to jump and climb and go through tunnels. This was *fun*. Hannah loved class, but as usual didn't always do what Mom or her Agility instructor wanted her to do. There are endless distractions around the training ring, and Hannah is adept at finding every toy or ball in the room. But she had a natural flair for Agility; and despite the fact that Mom is not quite an athlete, we entered an Agility trial. It was fun—no nervousness on Hannah's part and very little from Mom. Hannah successfully completed her Novice Agility title and Novice Agility Jumper title at the grand age of eight. She is now supervising the training of the younger Weimaraner, Mack, who shares her enthusiasm for Agility. Hannah is a happy dog who has a perpetual smile on her face. She enjoys running around her backyard, chasing squirrels, and playing with her toy poodle.

And every night Hannah climbs into the recliner with me to enjoy a little pampering and catch a few winks. She has spent the day ruling over the backyard and her other dogs. The Boss will be up early to make sure that everyone behaves and that the proper amount of barking is done at the garbage men.

MARY SIMPSON

32

SASHA
("SASSY DOG")

Hello there! I'm a German shepherd mix. My mom isn't sure what I mixed with exactly—maybe Labrador retriever or collie.

I was born in Effingham County about two years ago. I have been living with my mom for about a year and a half. My mom decided to get a dog so she would feel safer at home by herself. So she went with a friend to PetSmart on Saturday, April 19, 2003. I was one of the lucky ones! Apparently I was a week away from death row. Can you believe it? My foster mom sure did a great job of taking care of me; I still go up and say hello to her every time I see her at the Saturday pet adoptions.

It took a while for us to get used to being together, my mom and I. She learned a lot. At first I wasn't allowed on the furniture or the bed. I knew this wouldn't last long, though. Now I can get up on the couch and we share the bed. I even have my very own chair. It's comfy, too.

I've even conditioned her to feel guilty for leaving to go to work each morning. I think she should stay home with me all the time, but she keeps telling me that she has to go get money so she can buy me toys. Just as soon as she starts getting ready, I look really sad, put my head down, and go to my chair. I usually give a "harrumph" and a heavy sigh. (I don't think that she was counting on the guilt-trip thing when she got me.)

We live near Daffin Park, and in our neighborhood there are lots of friends for me to play with. Just ask Molly or Jackson (my secret crush.) I'm also a great jumper; if you come to visit us, I will show you. I just might try to touch your eyeball with my wet nose (very gently, of course). Jumping is one of my very favorite things to do. One day, I just know I'm gonna make it up one of our crepe myrtles or sweet gums. I know I can catch a squirrel, I just know it! But it's sure hard to get up those trees wearing a leash.

I'm also a good sniffer. Last winter I almost inhaled the entire floor when there was an opossum under our house. That was great fun for me—sniffing, scratching, barking, sniffing some more. Not so much fun for my mom, though.

One day I want to be a therapy dog. I will be a good one, too. I just love people. I'm trying to keep my jumping to a minimum, and only when it's all right to do so. I have graduated from my obedience classes, and I'm working on my therapy dog certificate. It's a lot of work to be such a good dog.

My mom thinks she's the lucky one because she got to take me home that day; but I know who the actual lucky one is—me!

SASHA

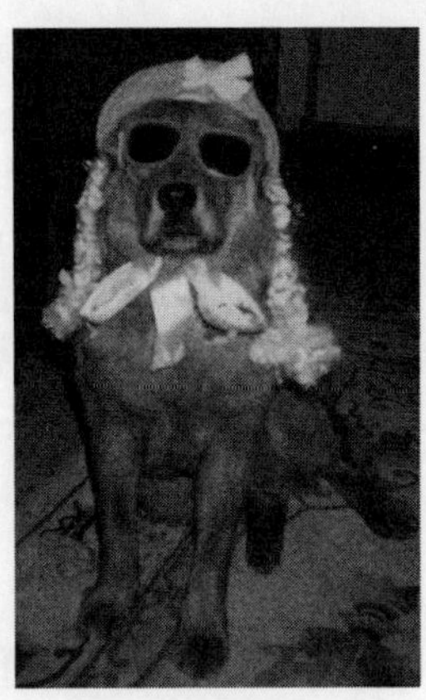

RUSTY

"Mom! I need you to pick me up from school!"

My daughter's request over the phone came as a surprise and filled me with a sense of dread. Why couldn't she catch the bus home from school?

"Just come get me, Mom! They don't allow pets on the bus."

Now, that's strange since I didn't remember her going to school with a pet.

When I arrived in the pouring rain at Shuman Middle School, the only ones standing outside waiting were my daughter, Erika, and a teacher holding a small, furry ball. As I pulled my van up to the curb, Erika hopped in the front seat, the teacher reached to open the back door, threw the puppy in, yelled "Thanks so much, Mrs. Hom!" slid the door shut, and waved good-bye.

Thus began Rusty's life with us. Shuman Middle School is located near a cemetery and, sad to say, some people also consider it a last stop for their unwanted pets. Hoping for a handout, Rusty had been hanging around the school, but ended up making a nuisance of herself.

One of our family dogs had passed away recently, and I had told Erika that the next dog we would get would be a "three-year-old, male golden retriever that is already trained." When I glanced back at this shivering ball of fur that fateful afternoon, I gave my daughter a questioning look. Her answer was simply, "Well, he's brown!"

Not only was Rusty not a golden retriever, she was also not a male and she was very young. Her initial visit to the vet confirmed that she was part chow and part something brown. She is very sweet tempered, and was very easy to train. She fit in well with our other dogs and cat and so, even though she wasn't a golden, we decided to keep her. And even I will admit eight years after she joined our menagerie, she's a pretty good dog and is definitely smarter than the goldens!

One of her favorite hobbies is watching the squirrels play in our yard. She would really love to catch one one of these days, although I don't know what she would do if she ever did. She has even gone so far as to watch the squirrels from the upstairs bedroom window, then climb out the window and around on the roof chasing them. After they jump to a nearby tree to get away, she simply trots to the back side of the house, takes a flying leap off the roof, gracefully lands on the deck, and waits by the door to be let back in the house. I'm sure it's disconcerting for our neighbors to glance out their windows and see this sixty-pound dog (which from a distance sort of looks like a big squirrel) running around on the roof.

Rusty became the alpha dog when our two goldens passed away, and she has really relished the attention. My husband became very attached to her and so, when Erika moved out, she had to get her own dog, because the brown dog stayed with us.

LISA HOM

MOLLIE

My husband and I first saw Mollie at a health fair we were at as part of a local therapy dog chapter. We had gotten our first dog from a dog rescue organization called "Second Chance." They had just acquired another Collie that they wanted us to see. She was in terrible shape. She had no hair on her tail, and most of her body had to be shaved down because of her being full of mats. The many areas of skin that were visible revealed terrible sores covering too large a percentage of her body, especially her legs and feet. But what really struck me about her was that as bad a shape as she was in, that naked little tail just wagged constantly.

Apparently this dog had been rescued by animal control from the "home" she was in, and the officer contacted Second Chance. She had been locked out in a backyard full of trash and filth, without adequate water, shelter, food, or basic care and attention. The owners repeatedly would leave her out there while they went on trips and vacations. The story is that occasionally a neighbor would throw some scraps over the fence to her. That was pretty much the extent of her care and being part of a family.

Finally someone reported the situation to animal control. When they checked on the complaint, again the owners were away on vacation, and they found a very sick and weak collie in the yard with another dog that had already died, who knows how long ago. Mollie had kept hanging on for a miracle she believed would somehow come to her. Animal control and Second Chance did not think that poor Mollie would make it, or that if she did, they would have to put her to sleep because of her extremely poor condition. Not only was she starved, dehydrated, and full of mats, sores, and infection, but also had heartworm and a thyroid condition. Her canine teeth and front teeth were all worn down to nubs from trying to chew through the fence that held her prisoner, and from chewing on her own matted hair. But she was so loving and determined that they decided to give her a chance, methodically taking care of one problem at a time.

Soon after I met Mollie at the health fair, Second Chance needed to temporarily foster out some of their dogs. Mollie had been stabilized, but was a good way from being ready to be adopted. Because I had previously adopted a collie from them and they had confidence in my ability to care for her, they asked me if I would be willing to take her for a couple of weeks.

Needless to say, we just fell so in love with this sweet, unassuming, always loving little soul, that she never left. Our other dog, Belle, took right to her and was happy to show her the ropes (including that she would be able to come back in the house when she went outside). The two cats that have been accepting of Belle's existence—though careful to avoid "collie cudees" at all costs—accepted Mollie as if she had always been part of the family.

It has been almost a year since Mollie joined our lives, and we are so happy to be able to give both our dogs the kind of life they deserve. We are blessed that they are part of our family now, living in the house with us, sleeping on the bed and the couch, and that they are groomed and well cared for. We have "family activities and outings" with the dogs, and Mollie has learned she can do things she never thought she could. She is now happy, healthy, and content. Like her sister, Belle, she is a certified therapy dog, visiting people in hospitals, nursing homes, hospice, battered women's shelters, and taking part in school dog safety programs and read-to-a-dog programs. She is not the type to hold a grudge, but only to freely give what she has to anyone that may benefit from her special gifts of unconditional love and forgiveness.

TIM AND KATHY LORENZ

40

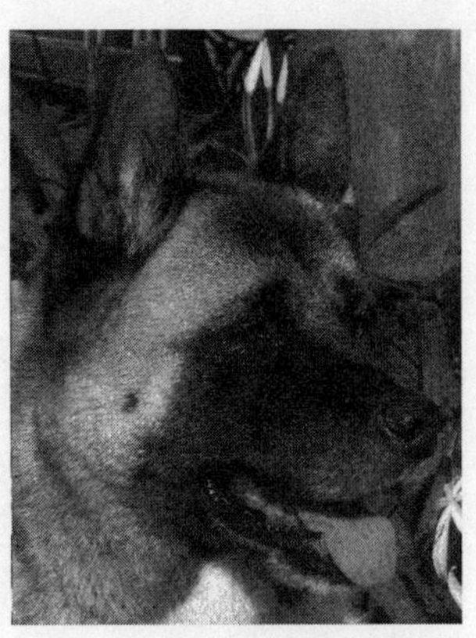

KIDAI'S TAKARA
SUMMER SUNSET
("TAKARA," "TK")

I am a gorgeous eight-year-old Akita, a canine of Japanese descent, not seen around these parts very often. When I'm out and about, people stop to inquire what kind of mixed breed I am. I have been truly insulted! I was originally one of eight pups out on a farm in Upstate New York. I remember I was having fun with my litter mates, when this old guy came along and decided that I needed a new home. I didn't go easily though. I was dragged into this thing with wheels that I "blessed" on my way to my new suburban home. The old fella thought I was an intelligent, loyal, and trainable breed. He must have read the wrong dog book. I am an independent Akita bitch and proud of it.

The house he took me to was nice with a large backyard and a fenced run all my own, but I was *lonely* for my litter mates. I soon forgot all about them. He started with all these sit, down, come, and heel comands and the big one, "speak." This was supposed to be my communication back to my master to go outside and not pee on the nice rug (did it anyway). I even had to speak for my food. As I got a little older, I was allowed to leave my "run" to roam the rest of the yard,

41

with me wearing this funny collar and with a lot of odd-looking flags sticking up all around the yard. Oh boy, this was my chance to see the rest of the neighborhood. My master kept saying no and shaking these flags, but it didn't make any sense to me. Off I went charging the line when I heard my collar buzzing, and then, all of sudden, I felt a shock. Ouch! Invisible fence. Boy! You do sure learn quickly.

Well, as you might have guessed, I grew up and went on to obedience training classes. I was smart, but really didn't want to participate. I did well enough though that I became certified as a pet therapy dog. Unfortunately, Akitas have a bad reputation as aggressive dogs and, therefore, I am not accepted everywhere. I will defend my territory and family, but my personality is sweet and lovable when you get to know me.

My folks were both show dogs. So, yes you guessed it, my master decided that conformation training was the way to go. Now wouldn't you have thought that I would have been able to meet a better class of "dog" here? They were boring, and the others in the class were, well, "dogs." At least my master gave me liver treats that were used in training. I went to several shows, even with a handler, but I guess I just wasn't pretty enough. Finally, I gave it all up. A few years later, my master retired and moved both of us to Savannah, Georgia.

My life in the South started out sluggishly, and my master decided that I was lonely and needed a companion. You should see what he brought home. He found a one-year-old Chihuahua–Doberman pinscher, a true mixed breed, through the Save-A-Life program.

He was kind of a cute, but scrawny, eight-pound creature that darted around and jumped all over the place. Why would they do this to me? His name is Pecos Pete. I outweigh him ten to one. Boy, he sure is quick. He's been taking all my raw hides and even confiscating my beloved bunny that I've had since I was a pup. Now his favorite pastime is biting my ear. I wasn't sure if this was going to work very well at all. I thought that I would make him minced dog by the time I was through with him.

Well now it's been a couple of years since we moved down South. Can't say I miss the snow, and I've adjusted to the hot, humid weather. Most of all, I sure do like Pete. Not *lonely* any more.

TAKARA

43

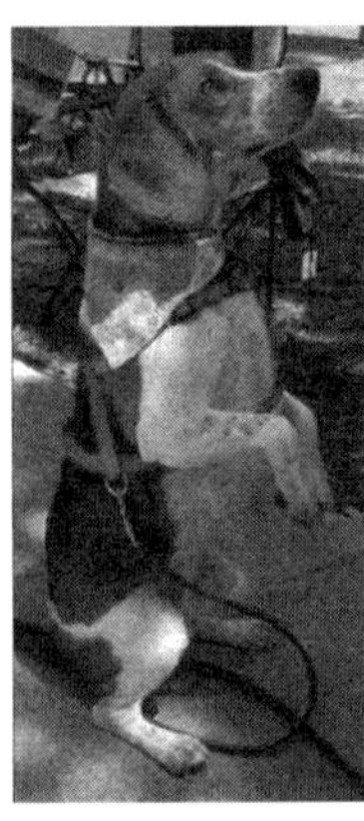

ELLABELLE

At an early age I rode home with Jones and Miss Deborah from rural Bryan County. "Ellabelle"—that will be the puppy's name said Jones as we passed through the town. My new home in midtown Savannah came complete with three other "citified" hunting dawgs: Maggie, Molly, and Lefty—all worthy of their own stories. On a number of occasions, following our hunting instincts, my pack and I have made the acquaintance of a number of good souls and dog lovers during some dramatic escapes. Thanks to those good souls and our collars, we never spent the night in the pokey. The couch is more my speed.

ELLABELLE

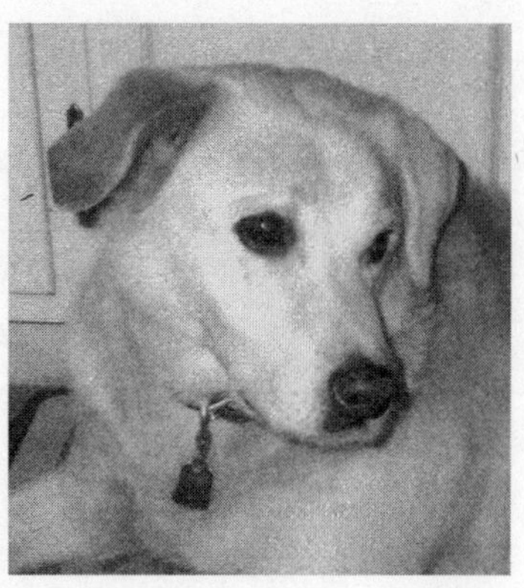

BEAR

July 7, 2004

Dearest Nancy,

This will be the saddest letter I'll ever have to write you. Beautiful Bear has left us. It was Friday, July 2, 5:15 P.M.

The frolicking mischievous puppy who ripped pants off of clotheslines and chewed up motorcycle seats with his buddy Vincent became the beloved pet of six crazy children who subjected him to everything from surfboard rides to walking bridges of jungle gyms. He became the kindly old gentleman who let a new generation of children pull his tail and tug on his ears. Ever the perfect example in everything, he was calm and peaceful all the way till the end, and we now realize that he was hanging on by the sheerest gossamer threads, I think, for us.

We had been struggling with the decision for over six months. Last winter a vet said that it was time after a nearly fatal bout with something called Old Dog Vestibular Disease, but with special care of our darling my mother mainly kept him going. He couldn't get up or down by himself and, once on his feet, often fell.

With medications we tried to help the failing muscles in his back legs, but to no avail. Recently he'd really taken a turn for the worse, and after the initial painful call was made to the vet, ear stumbled around on a patch of grass while we waited, and his relief was almost palpable as he went to rest immediately. He fell asleep in our arms, gently laying his head down on his front paws for the last time, and looked just as he always did. I believe that sheer will power and his incredible will to please kept him going. As long as someone jumped to help him get up when he cried out or hand-fed him dinner, he would have endured. Ever the beautiful golden Lab, Bear will remain in our hearts, memories, and souls as his soul is now free to roam the ocean he loved in search of fish or tear through a park in search of a squirrel.

As all of us spent the Fourth of July weekend together, memories of what seems like long ago with a frisky Bear washed over all of us, from the day we found him to the Halloween night that we found you, and your incredible generosity to share him with us. Thank you, Nancy. He was such a treasure. We were all so blessed to know him and to have him in our family. My little son, Joseph, wants to know where his "Buddy, Uncle Bear" is. "In the heavens, baby, in the heavens," we tell him.

Bless you, Bear. Run free and enjoy.

ANTONIA HALE

[For more on Bear, see *Savannah Dogs II*, pages 238–41.]

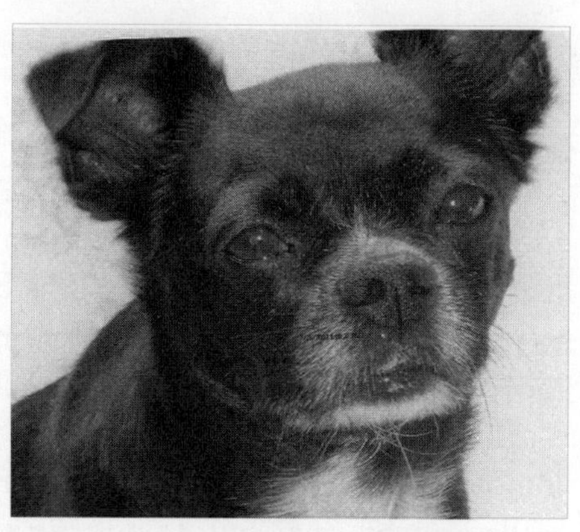

Gizmo Keen ("Gizzy")

It is true, I now live a charmed life, but my life has not always been so fortunate.

I was an orphan, and no one knows anything about my mother or father. My doctor believes that I am approximately ten years old. The first recorded history of my life began at the Humane Society of Chatham-Savannah. I was so lucky to be adopted by a kind lady. She took very good care of me for the first year of my life. She named me "Gizmo," but called me "Gizzy" for short. She made sure that I received all my puppy care and that I was spayed at the appropriate age.

Unfortunately my owner was unable to keep me. She was forced to move, and her new apartment would not allow pets. She boarded me for a while, hoping that she could work out the problem, but she could not. The boarding fees became too expensive, so she asked the kennel to try and help her find a new home for me.

Leigh, a young woman who worked at the kennel, told me that she had an idea to solve my problem. She said that she had a relative who was looking for a little dog like me. Leigh cleaned me up and took me home with her that night. When we got to her house, she made the call and arranged for me to meet my potential new family. I was excited. I might be going to live with a family with teenagers.

It was love at first sight. I became the younger sister to Thomas and Catherine. My mom officially adopted me in 1995. Then, in 1997, I was even lucky enough to get a new last name when my mom got married. We moved to a new home with a big backyard just for me.

Now my life is filled with fun and activity. I spend a lot of time chasing birds and squirrels. I have never really caught one, but I look forward to the day I accomplish this goal. When I finish my morning hunt, I enjoy a relaxing nap by the pool. I enjoy getting a lot of love and attention. I love all people (except the electric and gas-meter readers). I enjoy it when my family has parties because I am the center of attention. People are always interested in my heritage, and they try to guess what breed I am. When my ears perk up, I look like a Boston terrier. When my ears are down, I look more like the Taco Bell pup. Anyway, I am definitely a mixed breed, probably a Boston-Chihuahua mix.

I have bad a healthy, happy life. Dr. Lester at Island Veterinary Clinic on Wilmington Island, takes very good care of me. When my mom and dad go on vacation, I go to "camp" at the boarding facilities of the clinic and have a great time.

I can barely remember being homeless . . . twice.

GIZZY

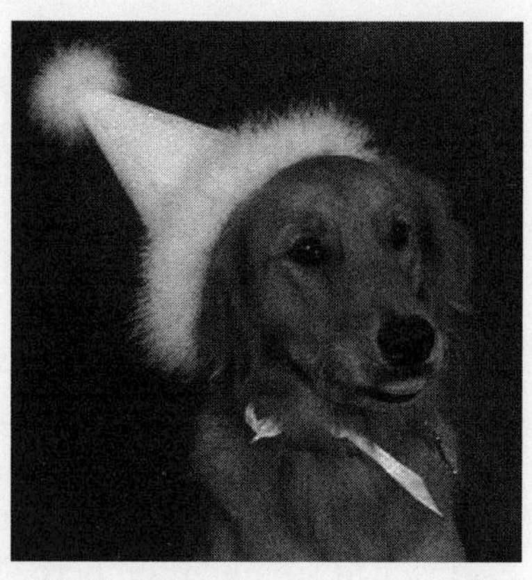

Daisy Mae
Kicklighter
("Dinky")

Formerly known as "Trouble," I'm probably one of only a few golden retrievers that can't swim! Now that I have your attention, I will explain to you my life with my past owner.

The man who had me before my new mommy and daddy lived on a boat. I was his "trouble on the boat," he said, hence "Trouble" as my old name. Having been a very mischievous and energetic puppy, I explored around his boat and dock, and usually ended up falling in the Thunderbolt River. After several rescue attempts via his fish net, I had decided that I was not a fan of the water. I seemed to wreak havoc on his small boat. Being bored to tears when he would leave me, I would chew up everything in sight. He would also leave me alone a lot, sometimes days at a time. So naturally I had no exercise or anywhere to go potty besides his boat. He wasn't so happy with me making my messes there. At that point he had stopped feeding me daily and would only feed me about every other day. This was no fun. One day he decided to get rid of me all together.

My new mommy and daddy were so lucky to get me, and boy was I glad. I was only about six months old. The first thing my new parents did was change my negative name from "Trouble" to "Daisy." Mommy and Daddy enrolled me in obedience classes; and when I had graduated from those, I then went on to the advanced classes. Every day I exercise with my mommy in the park across from our house. Speaking of my house, I love my new one with its huge fenced-in backyard, my own toys, and lots of treats.

I've had so much fun here. This past year has been a blast. My mommy takes me to the Doggie Meet and Greet in the park, and I have lots of friends there too. My best friend, besides my parents, is Bandit. Bandit is also a rescued dog. I went to my first Easter egg hunt with him in April and to a doggie carnival this summer. I have also been going to the beach. Mommy and Daddy are helping me take baby steps in learning to swim. I am still very scared, but I'm getting better.

I know that they say everything happens for a reason. I don't know if that is true, but I sure am glad that I am where I am. I'm having the time of my life.

DAISY

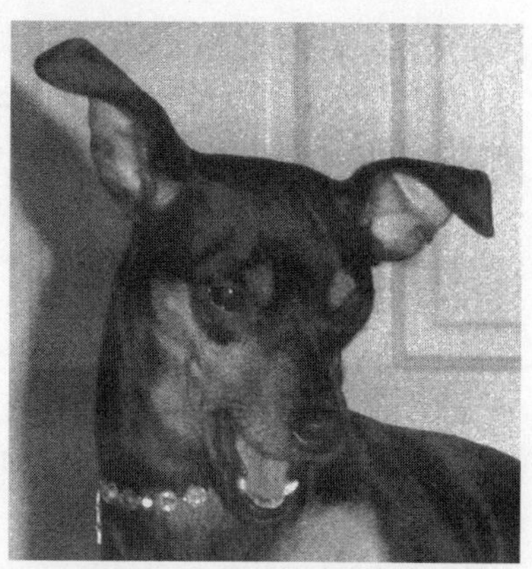

DARBY

Her entrance is always grand
As is her presence (for ten pounds)
She melts strangers into fans
Batting lashes, making rounds

Not just a sidewalk but a runway
When Darby hits the town

She tosses a knowing glance
Over twinkling crystals round her neck
Then kicks up the trademark prance
And leaves them wondering . . .

Heads Turn
Hearts Break

The other end of the leash
Merely holds the bodyguard
Or the press agent so to speak
The star is at our feet.

When Darby and I arrived in Savannah, I learned she was a Southern belle by nature. Her carriage was purely upper-crust during our first visit to the fair city, as she sat on my lap at a fine dining restaurant (outdoors). I instantly felt naked without heels, a big hat with a bow on it, and perhaps a Virginia Slim with a cigarette holder to complete the image.

So many strangers in City Market stopped to speak to her that I began to call myself her bodyguard. When she was too busy to stop for autographs, I saw the disappointment in the fans' eyes. I apologized and explained that she was quite busy and important, but appreciated their interest and hoped they would see her next movie.

Our routine walk around Forsyth Park presented the perfect opportunity for Darby to strut her stuff, and the sidewalk became red carpet in a matter of days. She wears her Swarovski crystal necklace and bats her eyes at everyone in the style of any smart debutante. Shameless flirtation is balanced respectably with coy shyness.

While carefully maintaining her dignity, Darby has a flair for the dramatic that sometimes borders on comical. She makes a big show of avoiding the drinking fountains along the center of the park. The fountain with the built-in dog bowl is the most horrible, and she keeps a pointed distance. A tragic drinking fountain accident in another life is the obvious explanation. Sometimes people see her making her wide circles (leaning against her harness and consequently walking sideways) and ask if she needs V8 juice. She is also suspicious of orange construction cones and anyone who is just standing around in the sidewalk when they should be moving along.

Darby's single most outstanding skill is her mastery of the feminine wiles. Seemingly born with the knowledge that most women require years to learn, she makes each man who crosses her path feel he is the only one on earth. She crouches down in an endearing submissive bow, something like a half-crouching sideways scoot when she encounters a particularly strong crush. Darby is a heartbreaker of the highest caliber. She leaves them feeling like a million.

Anyone who is in distress, whether it be physical or emotional, is given a strong hug. Her long skinny arms are more maternal than canine. If she feels frustrated, she heaves great sighs of annoyance, audible down the hall. If Darby is missing, the household puts out a search party and generally finds her wallowing in the sheepskin rug or under a down comforter in a bed somewhere; or, if she is feeling dramatic, cowering under a desk or a chair waiting for someone to ask her what's the matter. These are times that she gives hugs as well, but as a damsel in distress rather than a hero.

If Darby gets her way with you, she will sit on your head or your shoulders. In this way she exerts not only her familiarity with you, but also her superiority. Just sit still and feel special.

MARY MILLSAPS

53

I am seven years old. I have lived with Gail since I was about four months old. I had lived with three other families before Save-A-Life told Gail about me. The other families would say something about "too much time and trouble," and then I'd be sent away. There were a couple times I heard Gail say those words, but I'm still with her.

Gail and I usually play with the tennis ball before she goes to work. When I was about six or seven months old, I was waiting for Gail to throw the ball, but she dropped it. I thought it would be really fun if I snatched the ball before Gail could get it, and so I ran as fast as I could to the ball. Well, Gail was bending down to get the ball too, and the top of my head slammed into her glasses and nose. Gail screamed and fell back onto the sofa. I hid behind a chair and peeked out. Gail's nose was bleeding.

Gail got some ice and a lot of tissues, and went to work without even saying good-bye. She did say the "too much time and trouble" words, and I was scared I might have to leave. I finally fell asleep and forgot about the incident until Gail came home.

I could tell by the sound of Gail's footsteps that it had not been a good day. I hid in the back of my crate and moved very slowly when she opened the gate. Gail just lay on the sofa and told me to go away whenever I brought her a toy. She had taken off her glasses, but it looked as if she still had them on. Her nose was purple and green, too.

I kept waiting to be sent away, but Gail kept me, this time.

I was sure I'd lose my home when we evacuated because of Hurricane Floyd. All I remember is that Gail was real nervous and packed her things and mine. I was so excited about going on a trip.

After about seven hours on I-16, our caravan of six cars had driven only to Swainsboro. It was dark and scary. Our group pulled off the highway, and the people met on the side of the road to decide which route to take to Atlanta.

Gail told me to stay in the back seat, but I thought it would be cool to sit in the driver's seat. Longer legs and I'd be driving! Then I felt a slight breeze and realized the window was open. I could jump right out the window and join Gail and the others. Wouldn't they be surprised!

So I jumped out the window just inches from heavy traffic. Gail's friend saw me and came running toward me. Gail turned around and said a bunch of words, including "too much time and trouble."

Gail dragged me back to the car, pushed me into the back seat, and told me to *stay*. After another six hours, we made it to our friend's house in Lawrenceville. Gail told everyone what I did, but she didn't send me away like the others did.

No matter how much time and trouble I am, I guess I'm also one lucky dog.

SASS

Coco Chanel ("CC")
AND
China Girl ("China")

My name is China Girl, but my parents and friends just call me "China." I am pictured here with my sister, Coco Chanel, but everyone calls her "CC" for short. We are purebred Maltese puppies, and were born April 30, 2004, in Little Rock, Arkansas.

I bet you're wondering how we got to Savannah. Well, that's quite a story. My mom, Tomi Nelsen, had been looking for a puppy like me ever since she and my dad, Peter, moved to Savannah from California in February. My dad wanted to surprise her with me while she was out of town on vacation last month, so he called twenty-six breeders around the country just to find me. When my owner sent my photo to Dad, he thought that I was perfect. He showed my photo to his colleagues at Cora Bett Thomas Realty Company; and his managing broker, Elaine Seabolt, said that she would love a puppy like me too. Boy, was she in luck. CC was also looking for a home. When we found out that we were going to live in the same city together, we were so excited.

Elaine's husband—Uncle Randall, as I now call him—flew all the way to Little Rock just to pick us up since the weather was too hot to let us fly on our own. We were so happy that he was there to carry us as we had been nervous about flying all by ourselves. We flew to Atlanta, and then Uncle Randall drove us to our new homes in Savannah the next morning. I first went with CC to Aunt Elaine's house. Aunt Elaine was so excited to see CC, and I just knew that she'd be happy with them. They have two other dogs, Bailey and Gucci, and a daughter, Shannan, that CC would get to play with too. My daddy came to pick me up at Aunt Elaine's. He was so tall that I thought a giant had come to take me, but when I saw how loving he was, I liked him right away. He told me that he had tricked Mommy and told her that he had to run out to meet with a client, so when he brought me home that morning she was so surprised that she started crying and kissing me all over. I just knew I'd found a good home too.

Both CC and I are growing, and we both like to chew on our toys and run around. But don't let that fool you; we love to cuddle too. My mom and Cousin Shannan take us together to Forsyth Park, where we love to chase each other in the grass. The tourists like to take our photos too. They must think that we're a part of the history here, which is funny since we've only been here a short time. Now, however, that we are settling into life in Savannah, we are well on our way to becoming genteel Southern belles.

CHINA GIRL

58

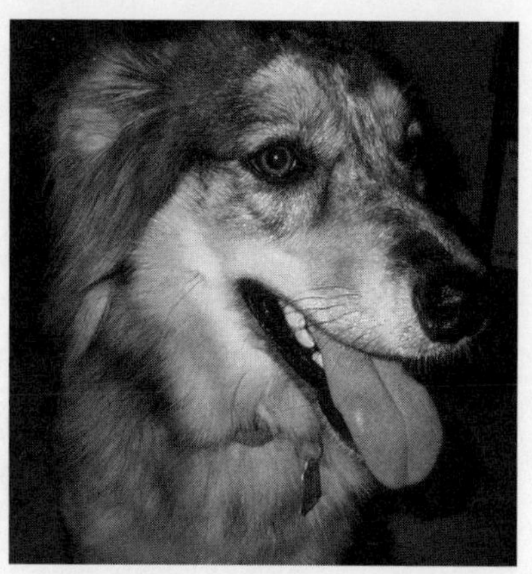

Cough! Cough! Oh, no, kennel cough! I'm told this is a "kill shelter" in Alabama and they'll put me to sleep tomorrow if I don't stop coughing. Who's that lady that's looking at me? Is it Trish James from Second Chance Dog Rescue? Did she come to save me? Oh, I hope so; I'm only four months old and too young to die.

Hurray! I'm leaving this shelter with that kind lady. When we got to her house, she e-mailed some lady in Savannah and told her all about me. She told Yvonne Romeo that I was the sweetest little red merle Australian shepherd mix, but didn't have a name. She also asked her if she wanted to adopt me and give me a name. I posed really nice while Trish took my picture and sent it to Yvonne so she could decide.

The Savannah lady had lost two Australian shepherd mixes in the past two years and wanted a companion for her Old English sheepdog mix, Rags, so Rags wouldn't feel so alone now that the other two had left. There were three cats in the house, but I'm sure Rags couldn't relate to them like she would with a sweet thing like me.

The lady thought and thought about a perfect name for me—red merle, sweet, hum. Peppermint Candy, Candy Cane—that's it, Peppermint Candy Cane. So my new name was going to be Candy.

Trish took me to a veterinarian in Alabama who fixed me up with some medicine for my kennel cough, gave me my first puppy shots, and talked about having me spayed. I wasn't sure what that was about, but figured out it must be something to do with playing in water. The vet was worried that my cough and the anesthesia might not be a good mix for me, so I didn't get to find out what "spay" meant. Trish taught me to sit and started my crate training before she took me to Savannah ten days later and introduced me to my new "mom." I knew who she was right away, and I tried to live up to my new name. She couldn't wait to take me home and introduce me to Rags. When my medicine was gone and it was time for more puppy shots, Yvonne took me to her vet and I found out that "spay" had nothing to do with playing in water.

I'm a little over a year old now. So far I have learned to jump our four-foot fence (so we got a new six-foot one), scratched a hole in the new couch while chasing the cats, and chewed a hole in Mom's favorite chair. She's promised to take me to dog training, but she works and her hours are different most every day. I can still sit, and have learned to come when called; and I can do a down most of the time. I'm crate-trained and housebroken, but I'm basically just a happy-go-lucky puppy, happy that Trish picked me out of all those others in Alabama and brought me home to Savannah. Every day I bark at all the other dogs in the neighborhood to warn them that I am protecting my mom's house because she was nice enough to rescue me.

Yvonne doesn't call me "sweet" that much anymore, and I'm not sure why, but sometimes she calls me Candy, sometimes she calls me Candy Cane, and sometimes, when I'm really playful, she calls me Candy Cain.

CANDY

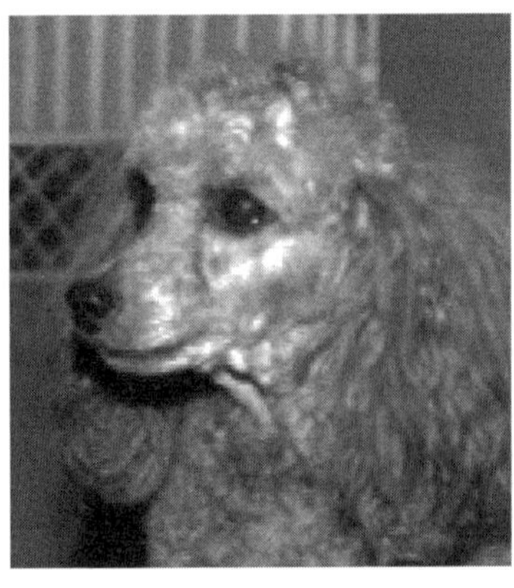

U-CDX Beau's Susie Que, CDX, OA, NAJ ("Susie," "Susie Sweetie")

Hi! What did you do this time? I was born in Tennessee. For my life's work I chose to be a devoted companion and performance dog under the care and education of a senior citizen and to relocate to Savannah at the age of three months. I am a toy poodle.

School has provided the learning challenges so necessary for my bright and curious mind. Heel, sit, down, come, and stay rapidly became a part of my everyday life. These were joined by "get out of the trash, drop it, quit picking on your sister, and what have you shredded now?" Advanced education has expanded my life to include retrieving, jumping, scent discrimination, weave poles, tunnels, teeter-totters, dog walks, and A-frames.

I love to travel. Meeting people and dogs, seeing new places, and being one-on-one with my human make a perfect weekend. I have earned four obedience titles and four agility titles. I even arranged extra trips to earn the scores needed for these titles. Near-misses get you extra trips.

As director of household activities I stay extremely busy leading early warning barking and door charging, polishing all feed dishes, putting the cat in his place, toy sorting, selecting humans for lap sitting, marking territory, shopping in trash cans, and major shredding. With my keen nose I can find *anything*; therefore nothing is really hidden from me. I eat anything except lettuce and grapefruit. I love chocolate, but my veterinarian says two emergency stomach pumpings are more than enough. My shredding skills are legendary and have resulted in two carpet shampoos, one replaced hearing aide, four new glasses cases, a fifty-dollar bill replacement, a substantial investment in new pens, one lunch-box replacement, and two vacuum cleaner repairs. I have created enough tissue and napkin confetti to supply a Mardi Gras parade. I even taught my sister how to shred, but her skills are far below mine.

Curiosity and courage provide exciting life experiences. When I was three months of age, I fol-lowed two Border collies out the door and into an airborne trip with a three-foot drop. The X rays were negative for fractures. At eleven months I discovered the firmness of the jump panel at the twenty-inch height when jumped without permission. Surgery and six weeks of crate rest have not dimmed my enthus-iasm for jumping. Last year I discovered that running down the dock and propelling myself off the end results in a wet landing. Since I don't know how to swim, a rapid rescue was required. No more dock- jumping without a life jacket.

It is my human's job to provide me with food, regular baths and grooming, the best veterinary care, daily exercise and education, and undying devotion. It is my job to provide snuggling, licking, toy-throwing

exercise, thrills, and laughter. And all it takes is twenty-
four hours a day, seven days a week, and all our energy.
   What fun!

SUSIE QUE

Mo

I am glad I came to Savannah. With my own futon in the sunroom, I can keep watch over my backyard for squirrels. Once I spy a squirrel, I burst through my doggie door in hot pursuit. Unfortunately, so far, the squirrel escapes. I return to my futon under the fan in the sunroom and cool off.

My life now is very different from my first six months on this earth. I was born in a foster home with lots of other dogs and puppies, in Halfway, Missouri. It was noisy with lots of activity. I liked to stay under the desk where I was safe.

One day I went with my foster mom on a very long car ride to the airport in St. Louis, Missouri. There she put me in a crate with the following note taped on it:

My Name is Mo
I'm a rescued puppy
I'm pretty scared even though
I'm going to a loving family.
PLEASE, be patient with me,

I'll try to be real good for you.
Also,
Thank you for helping me get
A
Second Chance of Love!
Mo

The next stop was the airport in Atlanta. My new dad, Ken, and my new mom, Mona, were there to get me. I was still scared. But then we went on another very long car ride to Savannah, Georgia. I was finally home.

During the next six months, I attended training classes and met many new people. Ken and Mona loved me very much, indeed. They taught me tricks and gave me lots of treats.

After I was a year old, Mona and I took the test for me to be registered as a therapy dog. It was not too hard. We all were very happy when we passed. Soon after that, Ken and I took the test and passed it also.

Now we go to hospitals, retirement homes, schools, and other places where I make everyone smile. I like it because I get treats.

When we take very long car rides now, we go to a place that has plenty of room for me to run and many different animals to chase. It is where Ken's mother lives. It is a very happy place. Yes, I am glad that I came to Savannah. But one day we went on a very long car ride . . .

MO

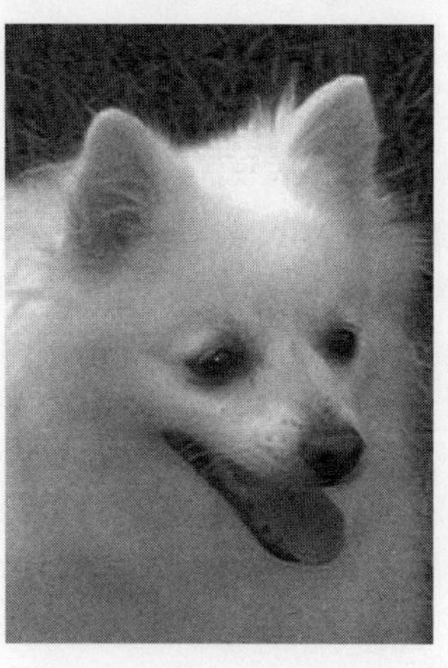

MINI

On this ride, Ken, Mona, and I stopped at a restaurant in Macon, Georgia. In the parking lot I saw another long-haired white dog. We sniffed each other, and then we each went about sniffing the landscaping for all the different smells.

I noticed that doggie items were being placed in our car from another car. We got back in our car—Ken, Mona, me, *and* this other long-haired white dog. She growled at me! Mona scolded her severely. That was that. It was certainly a very long car ride back to Savannah.

This new dog is called Mini. She is half my size and nine months younger than me, but she rules; she is the alpha female. We both like to go to Ken's mother's house, where we have lots of room to run and play. Mini has learned all the tricks I know, and we get lots of treats.

Mini is very inquisitive. She explores all things new to her. With my being the timid and shy one, I stand behind Mini cheering her on when she explores, "Go Mini Go."

Mini attended training classes and met many new people. Soon Mini and Mona took the test for Mini to be registered as a therapy dog. We were all very happy when they passed. Now we both go to hospitals, retirement homes, schools, and lots of other places with Ken and Mona. We make everyone smile, especially when we do our tricks. Mini and I like it because we get treats.

Mini likes to stay close to Mona, mostly inside. I like my futon in the sunroom. Yes, I am glad I came to Savannah. But one day . . .

MO

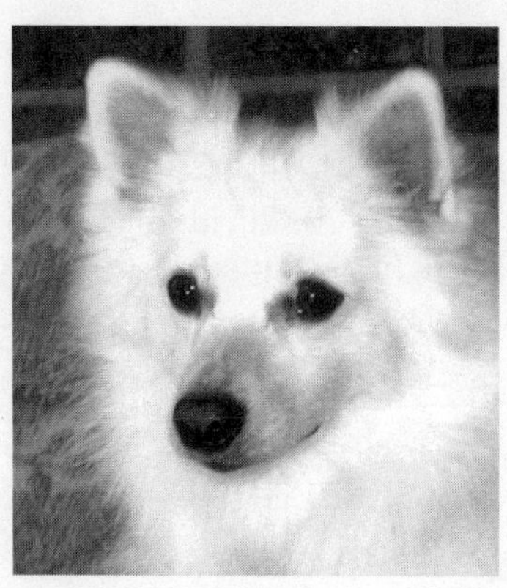

OLIVER

One evening Ken and Mona let Mini and me into the front yard of our house. There we found a long-haired white dog, only this one was a boy. He acted different, maybe because he did not know where he was, or he did not know how to act with others like Mini and me. He came into our house when Mini and I came in. We call him Oliver.

Oliver is half my size and two years younger than me. But he is very bossy—the alpha male. He has a great deal of energy. He and I enjoy playing tug; he can pull all of my twenty-eight pounds across the carpet. He is very noisy though. He barks a lot and even howls, which is a strange noise.

When he came he was rowdy and unruly. Now he is attending training classes and meeting many new people. He is learning all the tricks that Mini and I know. All three of us get lots of treats. Maybe one day he will be registered as a therapy dog and can go with Mini and me to visit people and make them smile. And we will get more treats.

Oliver did not like to go on car rides. He got sick. One time he got sick all over my backseat. It was awful. Mini did not want me to get in the front seat with her, but I did any way. Of course, she fussed. Mona scolded her. Eventually my backseat was cleaned up and I could ride back there again.

To help Oliver with this problem, Ken took him for very short car rides every day. Now Oliver goes with Mini and me on our very long car rides to Ken's mother's house. Oliver and I run and play all over the five acres. Mini is too fat to keep up, but she does try to jump us at the end.

Oliver and Mini like to stay close to Mona, mostly inside. I like my futon in the sunroom, where I can keep watch over my backyard. Yes, I am glad I came to Savannah.

MO

JACKSON
HOOKS
("JACKSON")

Dad never saw it coming. There were no warning signs, no symptoms. Just a simple statement from Mom: "Honey, I want a puppy." This started the exhaustive search that would change my life forever.

My name is Jackson. I was originally called Liam, but part of the joy of a new puppy is to name him. My parents had many ideas—Lucky, Lefty, A.P. But why Jackson?

Was it for Stonewall Jackson, the great Confederate general? Nope.

How about Bo Jackson, the legendary Auburn football player? Nope. Mom vetoed all football names (see previous A.P. reference . . .)

It must be Michael Jackson, the King of Pop? I don't think so.

Okay I'll confess. There was no great inspiration to my name. It came from a road sign on I-75 between Macon and Atlanta. But it could have been worse. I could have been called "Rest Area."

Anyway, back to my story. Once Mom decided that she wanted a Cavalier King Charles Spaniel, Dad began an e-mail campaign to contact breeders. He quickly learned that Cavaliers cost almost as much as a brand new Harley Davidson and the wait time is nearly as long. Things didn't look good at all. Then one day an e-mail arrived.

An outstanding breeder in North Georgia wrote that she had a puppy that my parents might want to see. She told them that I was bred for greatness. Both of my canine parents were champions in the show ring, and I would surely shine in the ring as well. My pedigree is quite impressive. There was, however, one little problem—a physical defect that would prevent me from being a show dog. I won't elaborate, as I am very sensitive about it, but I'll give you a hint—my parents should've received a fifty percent discount on my neuter.

With my dog-show career over before it began, I was now being groomed for another role in life—lap dog. My mom and dad drove to Royston, Georgia, to meet me and that was all it took. Next thing you know, I'm headed south to Richmond Hill, where I live with my parents and a big, goofy golden retriever named Cody (you might remember him from *Savannah Dogs*, pages 267–69).

Well, Mom got her wish. I am definitely a mama's boy, and in her eyes I can do no wrong. When I go to the bathroom, she gives me a treat. When I have one of those rare accidents on the carpet, she rescues me from Dad and says, "He's just a baby." Cody never got to sleep on the furniture until I came along. Now we both sleep wherever we want. And when Dad demanded obedience training, Mom decided to teach me "sit," "down," and "stay." (Sorry, Dad, that's all you get. If you want obedience, get a Border collie.) Mom says, "He's very cute," and I plan to milk this cute thing as far as I can.

I often wonder what my life would be like if I had been a show dog. I know that my brother is already winning ribbons and medals. But I have a great life with a family who loves me. I guess that makes me a winner, too.

JACKSON

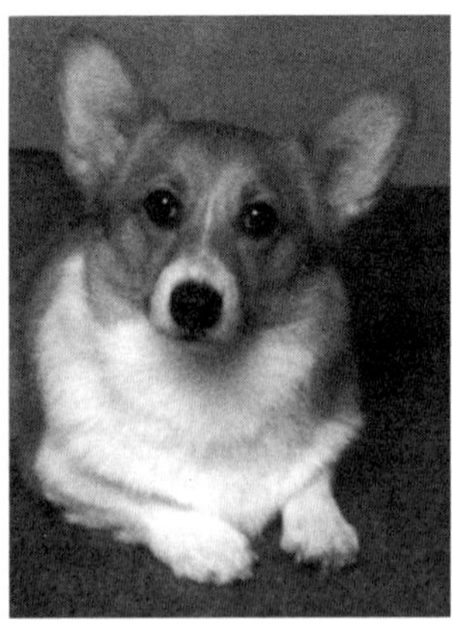

Artistry Alexandra's Dream, CD, UCD ("Sydney," "Corgi Boy")

I read the card on the cage: "This one-and-half-year-old female mixed Corgi was turned into the Humane Society because her owners didn't have time to spend with her [a common excuse] and that she didn't like children." Her soft brown eyes mirrored fear, and her large brown ears seemed too big for her. She had been turned in three days earlier. As director of the Humane Society, I tried to familiarize myself with each and every animal, and I asked the vet tech why the Corgi had not been given any vaccines or checked for heartworm. I was told that she wasn't planning on putting her up for adoption and that she couldn't get near her to euthanatize her. Several doggie treats later, the little brown dog was sitting on my lap.

After four months at the Humane Society, and no home in sight, I adopted her and renamed her Jennifer. She was without a doubt the smartest dog I had ever owned. When my granddaughter, Alexandra, was nine months old, they met for the first time and it was instant love. Over the years Jennifer and Alexandra were inseparable. It was Alexandra who—as she was reassuring herself that Jennifer wasn't old—asked if someday we could get a Pembroke Welsh Corgi. Of course my husband and I agreed.

When Jennifer died, I decided to wait awhile before getting a Corgi. Out two older dogs, a mixed Border collie and a collie, both adopted from the Humane Society, went into depression, never playing with their toys and spending a lot of time moping. Even the cats were unusually quiet. The house seemed like a tomb.

After a week I started the search for a Pembroke Corgi. First I contacted the rescue groups, but there were no Corgis available. After five weeks of looking for a well-bred dog, I located the Artistry Kennels in Fort Myers, Florida; and a week later, we brought into our home Artistry Alexandra's Dream, known lovingly as Sydney. Immediately the house hummed again. I saw a lot of Jennifer's traits in Sydney, and Jennifer has a unique personality. Corgis are active, busy dogs; and even though I had to push myself, we started walking and doing some basic obedience work. I have a chronic breathing and heart condition, and the walks with Sydney were pulmonary and cardiac rehab. It was imperative to teach Sydney what "drop it" meant since he would snatch up anything I dropped, including toads, lizzards, bugs, you name it.

When Sydney was seven months of age, away we went to doggie school for a basic course in obedience. Sydney loved school and that fall earned his CD degree in three trials, taking first, second, and third-place ribbons.

The following February I spent a month in the hospital. Sydney went to school to watch his cousin, Jenny, our second Corgi from the Artistry Kennels, work in agility. A friend who watched the classes said that she had never seen such a depressed little dog. When I came home from the hospital, Sydney never left my side. When Jenny left the house to go to class with my husband, he would look pleadingly at me as if to say, "Come on, Mom, let's go!"

I started to feel better and promised Sydney that we would go to class the next week. For a dog who had not worked in three months, he was so happy to be back in class and to be working as a team with me that he performed like a charm. There was a UKC trial in two days, and I told Sydney that if I felt well we would go. We entered for both Saturday and Sunday, and Sydney was "High in Trial" both days. An exhibitor's dream come true!

Bad health has reared its head again, but Sydney and I will be working together again in the near future—he insists. Sydney's devotion and loyalty are very strong, and his ability to entertain us with his antics is priceless.

Never did I dream that a frightened Corgi mix named Jennifer would lead me into the wonderful, wacky world that this breed creates. Sydney and his cousin Jenny are the best medicine I could ever have. They make me smile countless times every day. Sydney is my heart.

JAN CORBETT

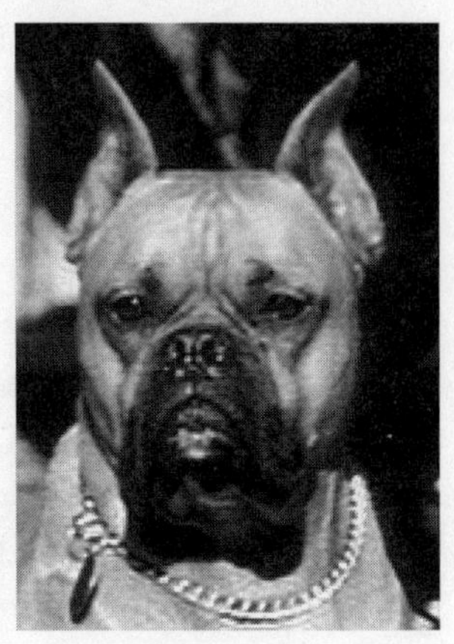

HARLEY MILLER
("PUCKY," "BUGSY,"
"H-MAN")

I'm a beautiful fawn boxer with a black mask and white markings. I was born in Fairway Oaks in Savannah on May 22, 1997. My grandparents gave me to my dad for his twenty-first birthday. This was while my dad was up at the University of Georgia. I became a University of Georgia college pup. College life was wonderful. I loved being one of the guys, except when they were upset with my teething and the loss of their tennis shoes, sunglasses, and expensive textbooks. I really thought they should be playing with me and not studying. But what do they know, I'm just a dog—or so they think—right? It was during those early puppy years that I learned all about the dreaded "time-out." I guess it had something to do with those textbooks that tasted so good.

I stayed with my dad for a year at UGA and then had to go back to Savannah and stay with my grandparents for six months. My dad moved into a new apartment complex and, of course, no dogs were allowed. While staying with my grandparents, I suffered from separation anxiety and my grandma had to take me to Carol's Pampered Pets day-care while she was teaching kindergarten. Boy, did I have a great time at daycare! I met so many new friends. The Labs were my favorite to play with.

Once my dad graduated, he moved back to Savannah. It was then that I realized that I had the best of both worlds, my dad and my grandparents. I wasn't spoiled at all. My grandpa has a floor covering business, a block away from Forsyth Park. I now stay with my grandparents at the business while my dad is at work. Grandma retired from teaching and works at the business also. I love to go to the park and visit with my friends and the SCAD students (they are really cool). I also love to chase the squirrels. I'm just not sure what to do with one if I'm ever lucky enough to catch one. During the day I usually go to the post office, Parker's for coffee and Cokes, and to the bank to make the daily deposit. I also enjoy going to get lunch with Grandma, but she usually makes me wear my seatbelt. I love lunchtime. It's my favorite time of the day! My favorite lunch is spaghetti and meatballs.

My dad lives in an apartment above my grandpa's business with his wife and her dog, Kirk. She's a great mom and he is a fun brother. He likes to go walking in the park, too.

My veterinarians are Dr. Max Cooper and Dr. Stanley Lester. They have helped me with some cancer scares during the past couple of years. So far I have been able to keep cancer away. It's nice to have doctors who really care about you. The girls in their office are super nice to me and shower me with attention. They usually let me sit in the chairs in the waiting room because the floors are a little chilly on my belly.

While at work I do a pretty good job of keeping everyone safe (when I'm not stretched out taking an afternoon snooze). I'm not fond of bikes, skateboards, or *cats*. However, I really love for children to come by and visit, especially my cousins Blake and Chloe. They love to play fetch with me and always share their hugs and kisses with me. I forgot to mention that I do spend a lot of time napping during the day. Work certainly wears me out. I especially love that afternoon nap between lunch and my midday stroll at the park.

My dad has spent so much time with me teaching me new tricks. I can sit, roll over, play dead, and hop like a frog. My brother Kirk and I hunt Easter eggs every year. My mom fills them with all kinds of treats. When I get into trouble (no, I'm not perfect, but my grandma sure thinks I am), I have to go to time-out and think about what I have done wrong. It doesn't take me long to win them back over. I shower them with sloppy, wet (and sometimes smelly) kisses that they just adore. Sometimes in mom and dad go out of town and I get to stay with my grandparents. They are so much fun and love to spoil me. I even get to sleep on their bed at night. They've told me that I am a bed hog and that I snore loudly, but I'm not sure I believe them. I really think they are the ones hogging the bed, but that's our little secret.

Well, I've certainly enjoyed sharing my story with with you. I'm such a "happy dog" and as you can see, live with a family that I truly love. My family really adores me and makes me feel so special. I wish every dog could have a life as wonderful as mine. I'm such a lucky dog!

HARLEY MILLER

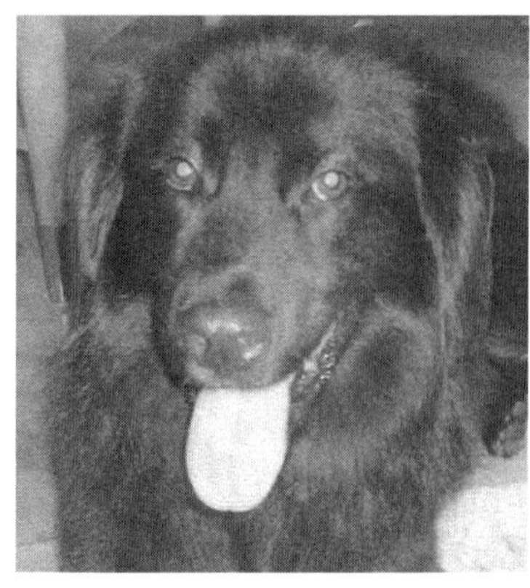

Dog's dog, people's dog, dog-about-Forsyth, I am fast becoming one of the most charming dogs in all of Savannah. It is a position that was a long time coming. My Labrador retriever–Border collie–Chow Chow pedigree gives me a surprisingly laid-back disposition, good begging eyes, as well as a self-cleaning coat.

I was brought to the Chatham County Humane Society as an extremely precious, cute, and adorable puppy. I was adopted, and, through a severe lack of taste by my adoptive parents, returned, multiple times. Because I had such a hard time getting a home, I was almost put to sleep twice. Did I mention how *adorable* I am? It is a sad story, but a true one. Sad, that is, until three roommates came to the shelter one day looking for (of all things!) a *cat* for Lee, one of the roommates. They already had a dog, Abel. They were looking for a kitty (Maggie, incidentally, is the cat they picked, and she's very cute, but she's still a cat), until Amanda, another one of the roommates, meandered over to the counter where I was sitting. She was helpless to succumb to my charms and bushy tail as Cindy, an angel working at the shelter, explained my plight in finding a home, and pointed out my finer features. That was that. Amanda is a long-time dog lover—no, dog obsessor—and decided that I would be her birthday present to herself. I'm almost two by now, but I finally found the right home. The rest is history.

It turns out that I was just the cure for heretofore mopey Abel. He is now my best dog-friend, and he has cheered up considerably since my arrival. Every day Abel and I walk Amanda and Abel's owner, Mark, to Forsyth. Many days we magnanimously allow them to stop for coffee while we lounge on the back patio of the coffee shop. I am quite the connoisseur of Savannah plant life, and once we get to the park it is strictly business as I go about sniffing, searching for only the finest trees and bushes, pausing here and there to meet another dog, or be fawned over by children, or to chase an unusually tasty-looking squirrel (if only I could just climb up one of those trees!). Mmm . . . squirrels.

Anyway, I often spend the rest of the day guarding the house at the front door or listening to cartoons from behind the couch or grooming Maggie the cat while Amanda is at school. Sometimes in the evenings I accompany her in order to protect her from the spirits at the cemetery where she works on a ghost tour, even though the way I stare at the dueling grounds makes her nervous.

All in all, life is pretty great right now. I meet new dogs every day, I get my belly scratched, and I get pushed across the wood floor (my favorite game) every evening. I'm looking forward to seeing the editor, Minnie, again, as I took quite a liking to her on our first meeting. Peace, love, and puppies,   BEAR

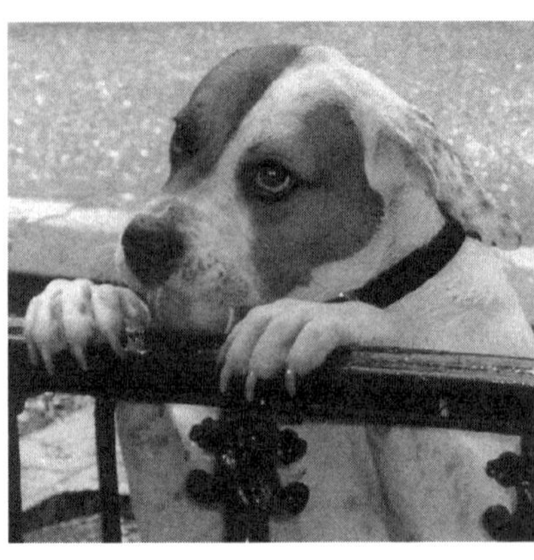

SADE ISABELLE GROOTERS ("SADE")

There were too many of us. Out of a dozen, only eight made it. Suddenly it was so cold and loud. Noise from every direction. I couldn't see yet, but it was the first time I heard my brothers and sisters. Everything once in warm, insulated gurgles now raw and coarse.

Those days all run together. The milk ran dry frequently. Mom never had much energy. One night the sky watered so long I thought we'd float away. We stayed in one spot until all of us kids were able to follow Mom by ourselves. Every day got colder and colder.

Then Mom died. She just fell asleep one day and never woke up. Us kids stayed together for a few more days until my brother got hit by one of those metal boxes on wheels. That's when the family began to fall apart. No one got along anymore. We all just went our separate ways.

I roamed alone. I had no one to keep me warm. My skin hurt from so much wet and cold, and food turned to ice. I was starving. I met a guy with wings called Pigeon, who told me about warm places and how to get there. He said he'd take me himself, but his wing was broken.

I started out alone, but soon met a great friend who climbed trees and had a bushy tail I thought was so cool. He asked where I was going. I told him I wasn't sure, but the sunshine got warmer every day, and that meant I was headed in the right direction. That's when Bushy Tail told me about Savannah.

We slept together under the Spanish moss, drank from the fountains, and played hide'n-seek in the squares. There were hundreds of other bushy tails! But when my Bushy Tail tried to talk to them, they would run at the sight of me. I felt awful. Bushy Tail came here to find his family, and I was making it impossible. I left Bushy Tail that night—the night I was taken by the humans.

I woke up in a cage surrounded by other dogs. They told me this was death row. I had two days left. I slumped to the ground and closed my eyes. She must have known. She came that day. I opened my eyes when I felt hers on me. Usually I would have barked and snarled, but I was too tired and sad.

She had real tears in her eyes when she saw me. I looked away. What did she want?

The next thing I know she's leading me out of death row. We walked into the sunlight. She knelt down and looked me in the eyes. I didn't look away this time. She threw her arms around my neck and whispered in my ear, "I love you, already."

I love my life. We practically live in the park, we're so close. We spend hours playing ball, eating hot dogs and puppy cookies, jumping in the fountains, wrestling with my little sister, Tallulah. We take weekly trips to the beach and swim in the huge, warm, salty fountain.

I try to do everything right. I bark at anyone who may be a possible threat to her. I bring her stupid, slimy ball back every time she insists on throwing it. I watch from my window seat to see that she comes home safely. I snuggle up to her every night so that she's warm, and I clean her face every morning.

I couldn't be happier with her, but not a day goes by that I don't think about my Bushy Tail. The other bushy tails still won't talk to me. They always run and make me chase them. One day I'll find him again. I hope he's found his family. I've found mine.

SADE

I am a two-year-old black standard poodle. I am rather handsome, if I must say so myself. I am very tall, about five-feet-one standing up. I'm very strong and little bit hardheaded.

My story goes like this. When I was a puppy, I was starved and abused. My home was not so good. I nearly died of starvation. My coat was brown, and my body was weak. My breeder, Suzanne, a pretty blond woman, rescued me and nursed me back to health. Now here I am, one year old and waiting for a new home. You see, Suzanne already had a full house, including my mom and my brother. Yes, my father is a tall, black show dog. My mother is a short, white, prissy standard poodle. All six of us siblings took after our father.

Well, as I am waiting a short blond woman named Deborah pulls up. She would soon be my new mommy. We went for a walk, and although I liked to go my own way, I tried not to pull. Deborah liked me, so we headed off to my new home in the country, a little town called Guyton, which was full of cats and boys on bikes. Yes, I like to bark at cats and boys on bikes, but

Mommy is patient. Mommy thinks that I am too thin, so every day she gives me a big pill to chew up. She also fixes my favorite meals—liver, sweet potatoes, and bacon. I also get to lick her plate.

Since I love to ride in the car, we pick up Shania, my best friend who is a six-year-old black Lab, and go to the city for doggie events. At PetSmart I also get groomed (a short cut, nothing fancy) and sometimes find another squeaky toy to add to my collection at home. My mommy and I are happy. When, however, she is mad about my barking and jumping-up, she calls me Pooh-Pooh, Maxie, and Maxwell. But I give her plenty of kisses, especially on her ears and feet.

I still have nightmares, but when I wake up I'm so happy to be here with Mommy. Never give up. Life can be good.

MAX

GINGER ANGSTADT
AND
BAILEY ANGSTADT

She arrived somewhat suddenly. As far as I remember the day started like any other, breakfast followed by a walk then settling in for a nap. Nestled against the sofa, I awoke to the clang of the doorbell. At the door was a nice lady who smelled like fresh air. She had come for a visit bringing her—a little big in the middle with a nice coat but different smell. She seemed quiet and reserved. After doing a few tricks (not impressive, I might add), she collapsed on the floor. When the lady got up to leave, she remained.

Life changed after that. Meals, walks, and even head rubs had to be shared. And the tricks—the tricks. How can you retrieve a little rubber ball that often? She spends hours doing that. Throw and retrieve, throw and retrieve. Ball, stick, Frisbee. It doesn't seem to matter. Frankly, I have never cared for repetitive exercise.

Why always first out the door? Sometimes I am actually closer, but that makes no difference. That body-check thing really sends me flying. Once outside she doesn't like grass, but walks only on flower or shrub beds. Who doesn't like grass? It smells so good!

Three weeks ago she started scratching her head. She disappeared in the tan metal thing for an hour or so and returned with no hair on her head. Talk about funny looking. Then I noticed how itchy my left eyebrow was. Scratching didn't make a difference. I stopped when I started getting the same looks she got before the trip. Of course we both got the goo applied; it was hard to rub off.

Food was the only area of common interest. She didn't like dry food at night so we now get some flavor! That canned stuff is pretty good. Boy, can she eat fast. Unfortunately she is no better at begging than I am.

Walking, walking, walking. My favorite outdoor activity. She starts off slow and steady. I spring ahead. Unfortunately she always gets a second wind toward the end, and I find myself following her tail. Last month we were out for a walk. It was hot and I was tired. As we neared the end, one of those moving metal things passed us with a little yapper at the window. The little yapper said some unpleasant comments to me; she dressed him down in no uncertain terms. I was impressed.

She is great with letting our owners know when someone comes to the door. She has taught me how to yell loudly, and we now guard the doors together. It's much easier with two of us. I never had a brother or sister that I remember. Now I always have company. Funny how things change.

GINGER ANGSTADT

LUCY

When my husband and I relocated to the Savannah area in May 2000, the first addition my husband wanted for our new home was a backyard fence. Unable to have a puppy as a child because of severe allergies, he was ready to make up for lost time, *now*.

I, on the other hand, did not even want a dog. I was quite content with my three cats. Besides, for the first time since my college graduation in '84, I was going to take a break from work, and was looking forward to a summer of leisure, reading books, spending afternoons at the pool, frequenting the local beaches. Little did I know how my plans were about to change.

My husband's cousin had owned an Australian shepherd when they were growing up, and he had always wanted one of his own. So when he spotted a "for sale" ad for Aussie puppies in the local paper, we had to go see them *now*.

We arrived on the scene to find about eight fuzzy balls of fur running around, yapping, peeing, and doing all those things puppies do best. My husband quickly picked the runt of the litter, a black-and-tan male. The owner, however, was saving that one for her grandson. My husband then turned his attention to the blue merle females that were available. He hemmed and hawed, picking them all up about twenty times each, unable to decide. I finally said, "For God's sake, they're all the same, just pick one so that we can go home today!" He decided on a blue-eyed blue merle girl with a funny patch over one eye. We originally called her Casey, but soon decided that Lucy was a better name for her.

Oh, but how quickly did her name change again. She soon became known throughout the neighborhood as Lucino ("Lucy-No!") and as Lucifer. Who would have thought that such a cute little puppy could be such a terror! She quickly dismantled my lifestyle. She was sassy, demanding, and always antagonizing my cats. Since I was the stay-at-home mom, I got all the joys of potty-training, first trips to the vet, taking her for her daily walks, and the list goes on and on. This was not the summer I bargained on.

Needless to say, Lucy and I soon became inseparable. When I went to visit "Grandma" in North Carolina, Lucy had to go with us. When we went for day trips to the beach, Lucy had to go. We even canceled a weekend getaway to Charleston because, well, Lucy couldn't go.

Since that summer we have added two more to our Aussie family, Cowboy and Georgia Blue. They each are just as special and rewarding in their own Aussie way. But Lucy was my "first-born" and will always own that special place in my heart. I can't imagine my life without her.

This year Lucy became certified as a therapy dog, so I hope that I can share with others some of the joy she has brought to my life.

LORI BARTO

# HAMILTON ("HAMMIE," "MILTON")

I'm also known as "The Big Poodle" and "He Who Jumps for Joy." I have a lot of things to be happy about, but it wasn't always so.

I was born in a kennel, and besides being fed and watered, I was pretty much ignored. When I was six months old, my life really changed. I was carried outside the fenced yard and put down in front of a stranger.

My strategy was to be like a boring sack of potatoes. I sat in a very bad posture with my head drooping down. The stranger spoke to me, but I wouldn't look at her face. She said, "Are you pretending to be Eeyore from Winnie the Pooh?" Her hands gently lifted my head so that we were nose to nose. I kept myself aloof; she saw no spark of interest in my eyes.

My plan failed. She put me in her truck.

New experiences piled upon new experiences—my first car ride (I barfed), my first time in a house (sofas—wow!—the greatest human invention), my first time on leash, the first time that I lived with a cat, my first toys.

I don't like to admit it, but I was confused. I didn't understand why people wanted to touch me. It made me nervous when the people in my new household came close to me. Much worse, almost every time we went for a walk someone I didn't know would come up and ask, "Can I pet him?" I always answered with sharp, anxious barks that said, "No, not a chance."

The best thing about my life then was playdates with other dogs. Most days we went to the dog park or met dogs in their yards for an hour of fun. I noticed that other dogs enjoyed having people scratch behind their ears and rub their backs. I decided to give it a try. Mon dieu! I had been missing out on some good stuff. Now pets are not enough—I ask for massages.

We haven't lived in Savannah very long, but I already have some great dog friends. One of them is Rudy, an Australian shepherd. He and I love to run madly about and then wrestle. Bailey, a Great Pyrenees, is another good friend. We mostly take walks together, but sometimes we frolic, or rather, I frolic and he lumbers. I also walk most days with Charlie, a Tibetan terrier, and Tillie, an Aussie. We make an excellent pack.

Life is good in Savannah, as long as I have my friends, my blue rubber ball, and full-body massages.

HAMILTON

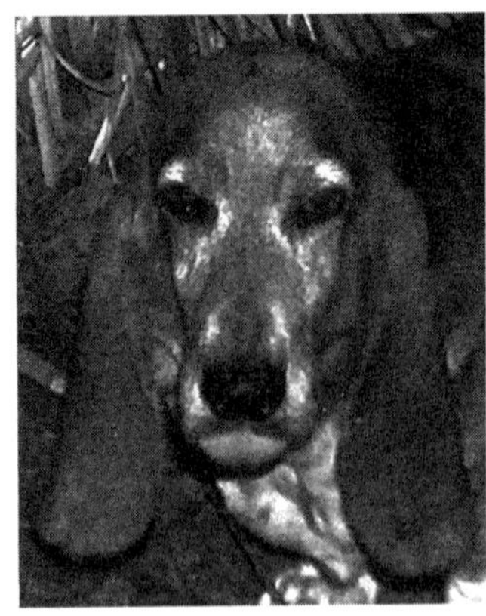

HUNTER

Hunter is an eight-to-nine-year-old basset hound that came into our household when he was about two years old. He was an AKC breeder that lost his mate through an unfortunate accident, and his owner gave him to us because we had previously lost a basset female on account of age and cancer.

Hunter has a very interesting personality. He's very cunning and tries to get away with things he'd like to do when he thinks you're not watching. He sneaks out of the yard for a walk around the neighborhood and for a snack of the outside cats' food. He disappears for about an hour and always comes back, but he tries to be inconspicuous by slinking along the fence and hiding behind bushes to sneak back into the yard.

He's not normally allowed in the house, but if he gets in, he will hide in a corner to avoid being put out. If you try to evict him, he goes limp, like a left-wing protester and you have to physically pick him up and carry him out.

He's a great early warning system. Anyone he doesn't know, and some he does, can't come on the property without his continuous barking. He's never bit anything but a dog brisket, but sounds very ferocious.

The highlight of his day is dinnertime, when I clean his bowls and give him his feed.

When he thinks it's about time to eat, he comes to me and starts to bark and wag his tail, and he doesn't quit until I give him his food. When I go into the house to prepare his meal, he thinks I might forget to bring it out, so he won't quit his "feed me" bark to remind me not to forget to bring it out to him.

He's a great dog, but is starting to show a little age; he has a touch of arthritis and requires a daily pain suppressor.

We love him. He makes a fine companion for our special-needs son and gets along great with the macaws and cats around the house.

BRAD BROADWELL

GRACIE

I was supposed to go home with somebody else the Saturday afternoon before Labor Day in September of 2003. Living in an apartment complex, my intended family put me on forty-eight-hour hold in order to get clearance from their rental agency before bringing me home. My future took a turn the following Tuesday morning, thanks in part to the Humane Society's stringent adoption policies for renters as well as the persistence of a Southern-born, Yankee-bred, young lady.

It was during the family's visit on Sunday that I first saw her. I had already been selected out of my pen to come into the waiting area for some playtime and interaction. Displaying my best behavior around the children, I sat quietly while they stroked my head and scratched under my chin. At the counter I overheard her explain that she was looking specifically for a mature and docile adult. As she followed the pointing fingers of the Humane Society employees toward the pens, I returned my attention to the family fawning over me. "Mature and docile adult?" I thought to myself incredulously as she came into the waiting area twenty minutes later with a six-month-old Labrador, "this girl is nuts."

Nuts, maybe. Prudent, absolutely. The following day she returned with a friend to visit the puppy once more, before committing to adoption. She looked away from the puppy's cage to think while letting her eye rest on something other than the object of the decision at hand. That was the moment she saw me. Her voice was kind, as she directed her friend's attention to my pen. Her hands were reassuring as they ran from my head, down my back, to my tail. Her kisses were gentle when she promised to return for me.

Though the family had a hold on me until open of business Tuesday morning, she went ahead and began the adoption process as well. In a somewhat underhanded move, she arrived at the Humane Society five minutes prior to opening. As a result she was standing at the desk the minute the family's hold expired, and hers commenced. We left together later that morning.

In the first couple of weeks together she tried many different forms of bribery, tempting me to divulge where I lived the first four years of my life, prior to that auspicious Labor Day weekend. I heartily ate the grilled steaks, but refused to give up my secrets. I admit it was a good life before meeting her, but that is obvious for I am healthy, well adjusted, love children, and adore kitties. In addition to being obedient and affectionate, the only time I raise my voice is to bark at the horse-drawn carriages downtown, and that's because they wear silly hats. Lucky for her I can easily sleep in on weekends and love to go on road-trips, which are exciting, but I feel like a dork in the car because she makes me wear a doggie-seatbelt when we are on the interstate. Eventually my history began to mean less, as we became comfortable in our new life together. Now she just makes up yarns about my life before she adopted me. In some stories I was a pirate, in others a thoroughbred, and once an actress. Like I said, she might be nuts, but at least she keeps it interesting.

I am lucky to be able to accompany her to work, which is doggie-heaven because there is a big fenced yard, sprinklers to run through during the summer, and my two favorite children. They are a constant source of attention as they explore the funny "camel-hairs" under my chin, my exceptionally long, red, eyelashes, and my whiskers that can be twisted into a mustache a là Salvador Dalí. I teach them to be gentle with animals and to show consideration for me when I am sleeping or not in a mood to play, which is rare but possible.

My favorite place we visit is my uncle's house in Charleston. When I go play with him, it is for a couple days at a time and it is like camp because we skateboard, go running together, play in the dog park, and swim off Folly Beach. He even taught me how to surf. Sometimes we head west and visit a fishing camp, which is great because there is a lake to swim in and woods to explore with my buddy Trucker, who knows the area like the back of his paw. But the best ever is when we go south and visit my grandparents and other uncle. My grandparents were a bit skeptical about her adopting a dog, until they met me. They all give me so much love that sometimes I think I can't be loved anymore, but then I nestle my head up under an unsuspecting palm and do believe I can stand to be petted a little longer.

All that is fun, but driving home from wherever we have been, with my head resting on the open window in the backseat, after a day of hard playing is when I am most content. Because I know when we get home there is food to be eaten, my friends the kitty-cats to be played with, and all my toys to be chewed. I also know that as soon as she climbs into bed, she'll say "Come on, Gracie" and give two pats on the covers, which is my cue to jump up and snuggle down for the night. She gives me a kiss on my head and tells me how much she loves me before turning out the light. I know I have dreams because she'll tell me in the morning about how I whimpered in my sleep or jerked my legs as if running. I have trouble recollecting these dreams, but suspect they have something to do with chasing squirrels in Forsyth Park, or maybe she was right all along and in dreams I envision my past as a pirate sailing toward a hidden lair on Raccoon Key with a fortune plundered from merchant ships.

GRACIE

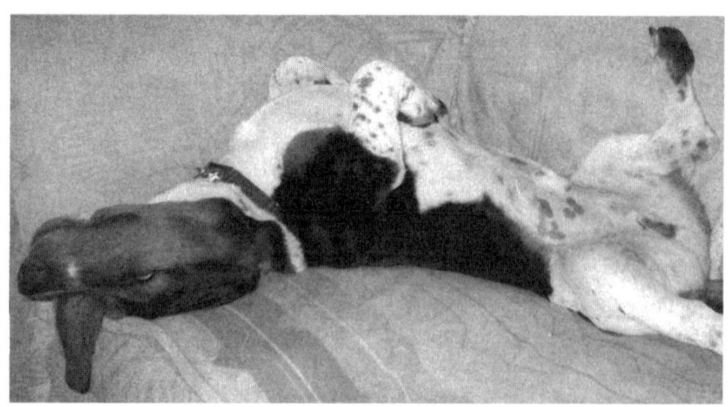

BLUE

For most of the ten years that my wife Kelly and I have been together, we have discussed adopting a dog. I have been a dog lover since birth, growing up with a Lhasa apso, an English setter, a shelty mix, and several black Labs along the way. Kelly grew up in a home with a cat, and as someone who is sensitive to pet dander, was apprehensive about adopting a dog. Further complicating matters, we are both active individuals who often travel. I am a pilot with a major airline; Kelly is employed by SCAD and is sometimes called upon to travel for work.

Another limiting factor was our home. For seven years we lived in Savannah's Historic District with no backyard for a dog to play unsupervised. That changed in the summer of 2003, when we purchased a home on East 48th Street. Savannah's Ardsley Park neighborhood offers many wonderful parks that are ideal for dogs. This move was the excuse we were looking for. We could no longer survive without a dog, especially if we wanted to take full advantage of our new surroundings—and fenced backyard.

Though we had finally agreed to get a dog, we were far from a decision on what breed, which gender, and how to adopt. I was determined to get a Lab from a reputable breeder. I wanted an active dog that loved to run, swim, and fetch, like many of the dogs I had growing up. Kelly wanted something smaller, one that was easier on the house and better suited for our small backyard. She was also determined to adopt a dog from a shelter or rescue group, thinking that it was important to help a needy animal. Our debate continued for several weeks until we found what we thought was the perfect solution—a basset hound.

It did not take us long to find Basset Hound Rescue of Georgia (BHRG), a nonprofit, volunteer effort to save abandoned and mistreated basset hounds. After looking at all the "available hounds" on BHRG's website, we were convinced that we were making the right decision. The last decision seemed to be the easiest—which dog should we take—but it wasn't. Kelly wanted a small female, one that would be easy to care for, especially when I leave to fly. I, of course, wanted a Lab in a basset body, someone that I could run and play hard with. In the end we both won. We adopted Blue (formerly "Thurgood," and "Jake" before that), a beautiful six-month-old basset boy. Blue (name chosen by Kelly) had two homes before coming to live with us. In his first home he was mostly neglected, and in his second, abused. Blue came to us underweight, underloved, sick with kennel cough and hookworms, and with a broken tail.

After a little TLC and with the help of the Southside Hospital for Animals, we were able to quickly nurse Blue back to health. Despite the trauma of his first few months, Blue is very loving, trusting, and friendly. And despite the basset reputation, Blue is very active and does not howl. Of all the wonderful dogs I have had, I believe that Blue is the most beautiful, and he is a constant source of joy and amusement in our lives.

JOHN BURT AND KELLY MCKEE

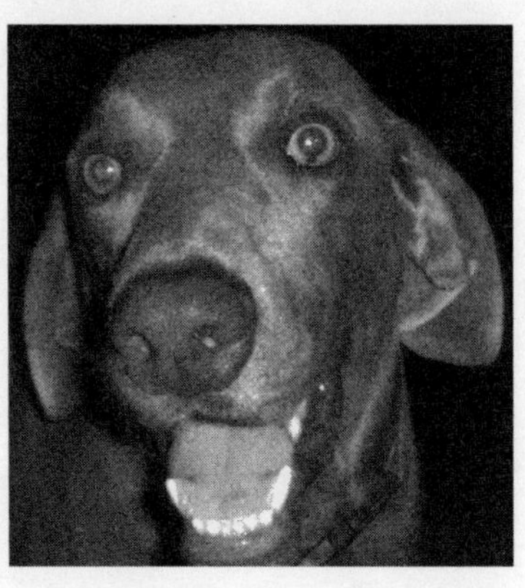

Charley Brock
("Monkeydog")

I am a six-year-old weimaraner who loves to go on walks, play at the beach, and laze around the house. As a new resident of Savannah, I am adjusting to living downtown in the Historic District by terrorizing the mail carrier and frightening tourists on my evening walks through the Savannah squares. One of my favorite pastimes is playing with my "brother," Leon, a seven-year-old black cat. I love to chase Leon and wrestle.

My most favorite part of the day is when the mail carrier comes and drops letters through the slot in the front door. I have to chew on every piece of mail. I know the mail carrier is scared that I will bite his fingers, but I would never do that. I just want to eat the letters he brings. During my evening walks through the squares, I can often be seen sneaking up on ghost tours and frightening people. I don't know why they are afraid of me. I am very quiet, and I just want to know what they are doing.

My parents are Chad and Amy Brock, who adopted me when they lived in Charleston. They give me doggie cookies and teach me new tricks. I know how to sit, shake paws, rollover, and stay. Sometimes people are scared of me because I am big and protective, but I really just want to play. I hope to make some new dog friends in Savannah so that I will have a playmate other than Leon the cat.

I look forward to the winter months because I love to snuggle. Chad and Amy gave me my own special blanket, and I love to be wrapped up in it. Sometimes I hide from them under my blanket, but they always seem to find me. They are very generous and let me lie in their laps, even though I am probably too big. I love to show my affection and be close to my parents at all times.

CHARLEY

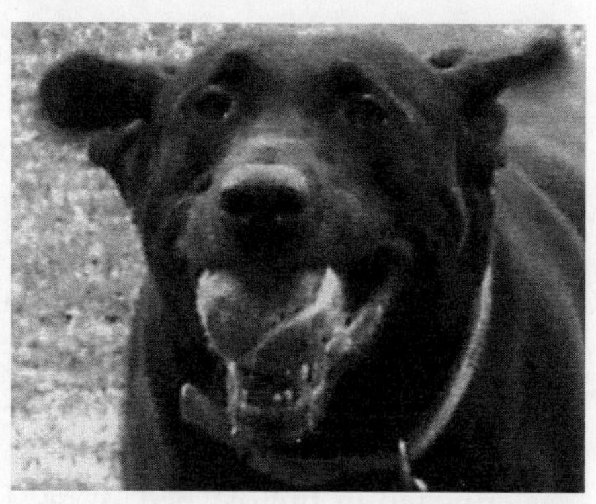

I didn't know what love was until the Chapmans adopted me. Two other families had fostered me before I even turned one, but I never seemed to fit in. No one wanted the big girl with a lot of boundless energy. I tried to keep my exuberance down, but it was so hard when I always feel like bursting. I can't help it if I'm a happy dog. Life is too short to walk through life when you can run instead. And I love to chew; nothing makes me happier than having a big bone to snack away on.

Then one day my life changed for the better. I met my new mommy and daddy. They had kind eyes and soft voices, and they seemed to really love each other, so I prayed that they would love me just as much. I wasn't worried when they put me in their truck and drove away from my old home. I could tell that the Chapmans were the best. They kept talking to me, telling me how happy they were that I was going to be their dog.

My new house is the best. I have my own place for water and food, and I can go into every room of the house. I even have two brothers and one sister. Although they are of the feline variety, I love them very much. There is nothing like playing chase, though sometimes Mommy and Daddy scold me for being too loud. I'm working on my inside voice. Mommy tells me not to worry, that it will come to me when I get a little older.

One of my favorite days was when Mommy and Daddy brought home our new bed. I must be one of the luckiest dogs in the entire world because I get to sleep with my parents; though I have to admit that it was crowded in the old bed. Why, I could barely turn around at night. Don't tell Mommy, but she likes to hog the covers while Daddy takes up so much room. It was tough too because Daddy would get a little irritated if I disturb his sleep. He works the craziest hours, but do you know how hard it is to be quiet and stay on my side of the bed? Nearly impossible. But this new bed—Mommy calls it king-sized, Daddy calls it the best investment he every made—is huge. Now even my brothers and sister can curl up on the bed with us without getting mad that we are invading their space. I can also move around a lot without disturbing Daddy, though I need to talk to him about being quieter when he gets up for work. But I do love to curl up on his warm pillow when he gets up and then snuggle into the covers. It's nice and toasty.

I love both of my parents equally. Mommy is so nice and soft. She's always giving me kisses and letting me have treats. Daddy is the best for watching football games then taking me out to chase the ball. I think my favorite time is when we're all home together and it's right before everyone falls asleep. I'm so tired, my parents are tired, and so are my siblings. It's the one time when everyone is quiet and I can hear Mommy and

Daddy talking together. It makes me feel all mushy inside knowing that we are all loved.

GABBIE

MAJER'S JUANITA CHIQUITA ("CHIQUITA")

Hola, amantes de perritos! Este es mi cuento.

I am a fourteen-year-old, black-white-and-tan toy Chihuahua. When I was adopted in March 1991, just three months after my birth, I was surprised to learn that I was not the only dog in the house. Juan Bandito, a fawn and black toy Chihuahua, only nine months old at the time, was already living with my owner. Bandit immediately succumbed to my charms and allowed me to take my rightful position as alpha dog. I taught him a few things about having fun. We immediately began chewing up our lovely wicker bed, but, of course, we were both teething! I was soon saddled with enrollment in the Pet Assistance League's PawPrint Dog Training Class. But I was not going to submit to my owner or to trainer Catharine Kelly without a struggle! Of course Catharine did turn out to be the alpha female, and she promptly designed the smallest pinch collar on earth. But it worked like a charm, and to this day I am the only dog in my household that sits, downs, stays, rolls over, and spins on command. Of course, I let them think I am doing this because they ask me to, but I really do these things for the treats.

About three years after I moved in, my owner brought home another dog, Achy Breaky Heart. He is a long-haired teacup Chihuahua and the biggest whimp you can imagine. I have managed to teach him a few things, but he is so fragile and his barks sound like a bird chirping. If I get too tough with Achy, my owner promptly downs me and calls me "bad girl." I much prefer when she calls me "pretty girl," but sometimes the alpha in me takes over. Because my owner thinks "you can never be too thin or have too many Chihuahuas," a couple of years later Tiny Tater Tot, a smooth-coat teacup Chihuahua, came to live with us. Tate is very shy, but she doesn't take too much bullying from the rest of us. She has that big-dog mentality like the rest of us! And just when you think our house can hold no more Chihuahuas, my owner came home in 1998 with Little Queenie, a smooth-coat teacup who turned out to be a teapot! Little Queenie is in training to take over my position one day, and every once in a while I let her pretend she is in charge. She has a way of imposing herself on all of us whether we want her there or not. But she is very lovable and even has Bandit playing around again.

My owner's husband, Rich, who is a great cook, always provides us with juicy bones to chew and sneaks treats to us when she isn't looking. When he works at night, we have grand pajama parties (usually just the girls) and we get to snuggle under the covers all night. It gives me a chance to protect my owner from things that go bump in the dark and from the monsters under the bed. For the most part I sleep during the day, except when I am outside chasing lizards and squirrels or trying to eat the goldfish food out of the pond. Sometimes I like to go into the garden, and sun and wait for my owner to come home. I always greet her, along with the others, with a wagging tail; and she always greets us with smiles, hugs, and kisses! Overall, I have a wonderful home and I don't even mind it too much when my owner makes us dress up each year for the PALS Halloween Costume Contest. My owner really loves winning the contest and spends weeks with my granny (her mother, Imogene) designing and creating elaborate costumes, so I tolerate the laughter from the judges and the hot, itchy costumes for a little while and am thankful Halloween only comes once a year!

Thanks for reading my story. Adios amigos.

CHIQUITA

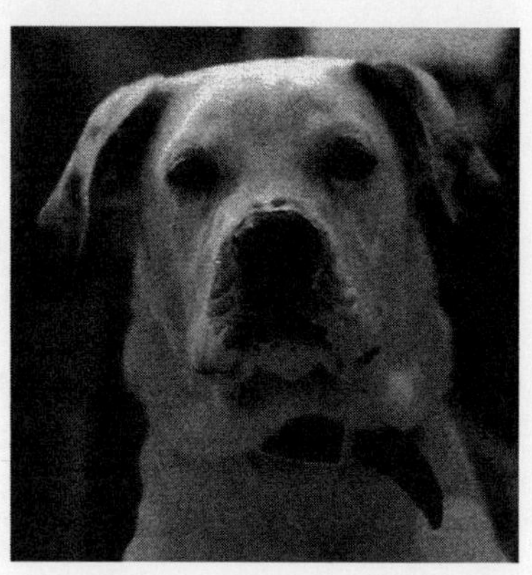

EMO

Emo, my nine-month-old American bulldog mix, and I are best friends. Granted, I've only had him for three mouths, but I cannot imagine what life would be like without him. Having grown up around dogs my whole life, I had a general idea of what it would be like to finally have my own. Believe me, I got more than I bargained for—in a good way. I now have a full-time companion. He goes with me everywhere, even across the country. We eat together, sleep together, and play together. In fact, the only real time that we are apart is when I am in class.

School presents a major barrier when it comes to spending time with Emo. This is mainly the reason why Emo only knows how to sit, lay down, and speak (although I am totally confident that he is perfectly capable of performing many other tricks). So instead of learning tricks during our quality time, we like to sleep or play. Besides food, toys are Emo's favorite things. But I am convinced that even if there were no toys, Emo could be perfectly content playing with the natural toy—the stick. Sticks are the only things Emo will kind of fetch, but I think that's mostly because he likes to eat them more than play with them. Actually Emo is not very good at playing fetch at all. He doesn't really run, but rather leaps and bounds toward his prey.

Another one of Emo's hobbies is exploration. This, however, has resulted in a few scary moments for me, like the time when he disappeared in my neighbor's backyard. After twenty minutes of looking for him, we organized a small search party and screamed his name across the neighborhood. About five minutes later, we discovered the poor pup frantically pawing at the lattice from beneath the neighbor's house. It appeared as though he had found his way in, but had no clue as to an exit.

Beyond toys and explorations, Emo, of course, loves other dogs. He has been accused of being slightly too friendly as he will approach any dog without care or caution. Once, however, the initial introductions have been made, the playtime begins. Emo chases and wrestles with other dogs until I am forced to drag him away. Even then, he tries his best to stay. He plants his feet firmly on the ground so that I cannot move him. It's almost like pulling deadweight.

Once playtime is over and we settle in for the night, I realize how lucky I am to have such a blessing as Emo. I am never lonely, and he never fails to make me smile. No matter how hard life gets, he is always there to offer his friendship and loyalty. Emo is very protective and makes me feel a little safer to be a female college student. In the end I need him just as much as he needs me. Indeed, I am looking forward to the years to come, sticks and all, with Emo by my side.

SARAH COBB

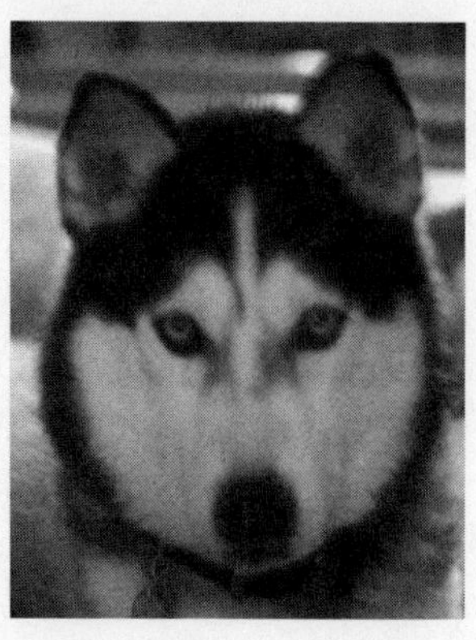

CHRISTIAN

It had been a bad summer. The worst part was having to put my beloved yellow Lab Beauregarde of Beaulieu (aka Beau) to sleep. I am really not sure exactly what happened to him. Probably delayed or cumulative injury from jumping off my second-story balcony in lustful pursuit of a cute neighborhood shelty. I thought sure I was going to find him severely injured when I looked over the railing. But there he stood looking up at me with a stunned look of awe. I would notice an occasional limp or wallow in his walk. The vet said there was spinal and hip injury. His status gradually worsened until on August 6 he could no longer climb the stairs to my bedroom nor hold himself up for any length of time. I made the painful but humane decision to put him to sleep. I sat on the floor of the vet's office, stroking his head as he peacefully entered another world. I was not, however, totally alone.

I had three other dogs to keep me company. My mixed black Lab, Perle (who came with the house that I bought), my blue-eyed black-and-white male Siberian husky, Bullet, and my streetwise little mixed terrier, Rocky. Rocky had been used to coming in the house for quite some time. But now I was ready to let Perle and Bullet in. The four of us continued just fine. I was spending more time with them, and they seemed to really enjoy it.

Bullet and I began to have early morning runs, which were quite invigorating as the fall and winter progressed. Then, on the Wednesday before Thanksgiving, I went out to check on him and he was dead. Two hours earlier he had been fine. The vet said it was probably a heart attack. He was approximately eleven years old. Even though it was quite upsetting, I surely must have been a sight in my nightgown, trying to carry a sixty-five-pound dog to a respectable burial place in his yard. If you haven't figured out by now, I am quite the independent type and handle things like burying my dog by myself.

At this point I was starting to lose faith in my dog-ownership abilities. Yet there was this nagging emptiness that led me to the Humane Society on the Monday after Thanksgiving. I had made up my mind to get a cat. I had decided to diversify my animal menagerie. I was telling the kennel worker about my recent losses. And what did they happen to have for adoption—a seven-month-old, blue-eyed, black-and-white, male, Siberian husky. He was quite shy at first and hesitated to come to the door of his kennel. But it was love at first sight; as soon as I saw him I knew I wanted to take him home.

Of course I had to go through the application process and bring Perle and Rocky in to be interviewed. Their Humane Society rules were quite strict, and it finally took a call from my vet for him to be released. He had to be neutered first, and finally, the week before Christmas, I was able to bring him home. He was still quite shy. When he got in the car, he laid his head on my lap for our trip home. In honor of the Christmas holiday, I decided to call him Christian. I will never forget the drive home in the dark with all the Christmas lights sparkling on Beaulieu Avenue with Christian in my lap.

As his comfort level increased, he became quite the roving fellow, finding numerous ways of getting out of my yard. Since he was easily able to leap over the four-foot fence, it was replaced by a six-foot fence. Yet this did not stop him. He merely climbed on top of his dog house and jumped the six-foot fence from there. I wised up and moved his doghouse. This did not deter him. Since elevations were no longer successful, he decided to go the low road and dig under the fence. I filled the holes with cement, bricks, and slabs of wood, and even laid wire mesh, perpendicular and secured to the fence. He even figured out how to unlatch the gate. Finally, after having to leave work a few times to retrieve Christian, he became an inside dog. I saw no reason, however, to do the same to Perle. (Rocky had since passed on at the ripe old age of eighty-four.) This was not accepted by Christian. He was not going to be separated from his woman. He made that very clear to me with a demonstration of the removal of my patio door blinds. I succumbed. After all, two is company and they both became full-time house dogs. That was 2001.

I eventually had to sell my house in Beaulieu the next year. This was very disheartening to Christian as he had become deeply infatuated with a younger Lab mix named Dixie, who lived next door. (Perle did not seem to mind too much as she was getting on in years.) I had the greatest real estate agent in the world

(Steffany Farmer from Coldwell Banker), who would patiently care for the dogs as potential buyers would roam the house. She patiently assisted me in search of a dog-friendly, safe-walking neighborhood with a house that included a big fenced yard. (I think she was secretly amused at my eccentric priorities.) We finally settled on Wilmington Park on Wilmington Island. Unfortunately Perle was diagnosed with bladder cancer the year we moved, and she too had to be put to sleep, in the same peaceful manner as Beau.

Christian and I have just finished Doggy School (Basic Obedience Training). It was quite a proud moment when I accepted our third-place ribbon at graduation. I am really going to miss seeing the gang: Daisy, Chewy, Alfie, Schlitz, and Oliver. So now it is just Christian and I, and he is truly the best friend I have ever had. We've been through a lot together, including a fourteen-hour car drive during a hurricane evacuation. He soon will be an official therapy dog, so I hope that I can share with others-in-need some of the joy he has brought to me.

MAUREEN DAVIS

Katie Scarlett of Paradox Farms ("Scarlett")

Scarlett was born on April 6, 1999, at Paradox Farm Kennels in Conyers, Georgia. Two veterinarians who were married to each other bred and raised long-haired dachshunds.

It was a sequence of coincidences, odds, chance, and timing that brought us together. During my childhood, boxers were our family pets. My first dog as an adult was another long-haired dachshund, Gretchen. She came from Dachs o Marshes, a former kennel out on the way to Skidaway. A Mrs. Youmans ran it for years. I had Gretchen for thirteen years. She died at thirteen from a ruptured disk. At that time they did not do surgery here in Savannah for disk problems, and nothing could be done to save her. The decision to have her enthanatized was terrible for me. Her loss was so traumatic that I decided I could never have another dog. I waited eleven years for Scarlett.

Life went on. I sold the house that had a fenced-in yard. I bought a condo with no yard, only marsh behind it. The closest I came to dogs were those that belonged to my family and friends.

Then, five years ago, fate was on my side. I bought another condo (this one with a small fenced-in patio).

It just happened to be a few blocks from the hospital where I worked as a nurse, and I bought a new computer. At the same time, a feeling began to grow inside me that I had to get a dog and it had to to be another miniature, long-haired dachshund. On the third night that I was searching on the Internet, I found a long-haired, chocolate-and-tan dachshund. I contacted the veterinarian in Conyers, sent a deposit, and planned to go up in three days to get her.

The day before I left, I went shopping and bought two of everything—crates, bowls, toys, and anything else I saw. I wanted her to have one for downstairs and one for upstairs. The pet store was sorry to see me leave. I was so excited to get her.

I also left many close friends, coworkers. relatives, and a significant other questioning my sanity. "This will not work out," "you are making a big mistake," "you will not keep her," "the last thing you need is a puppy," "you can hardly get to work by 7 A.M. now." I was pretty used to doing what I wanted to do, when I wanted to do it. I loved to sleep late. I just called them "doubters" and said, "You will see."

Scarlett was given to me on Staurday, June 22, 1999. She was ten weeks old. My life has not been the same since. It seemed as though I had been waiting for her all my life. I had planned to put her in a crate to bring her back to Savannah, but she just curled up in my lap and stayed there till we got home. Scarlett is such a happy dog. She has never met a stranger. She is full of love and affection. When I come home in the afternoon, you would think she is waiting for a rock star. She is happy to see me. She runs around, jumps up and down, waiting for a hug.

She was "home schooled," as I never got around to obedience class. She does not do tricks. She loves to play "fetch." Her version, however, is to dash for whatever toy I throw. She gets so excited that she runs to get it and, without the toy, runs back to be praised and petted. Scarlett has two toy baskets, one upstairs and one downstairs. She loves to play with her toys and carry around her stuffed toys. Many are as big as she is. Probably her favorite pastime is posing for pictures. That could be because her mother cannot get enough pictures of her. She has her picture taken for every occasion, and then sometimes, when I just look at her, she looks so cute that I have to take a picture. I feel safe in saying that next to the line of UGAs she has more pictures taken of her than any dog in Savannah. She likes walking and riding in the car. She loves to cuddle up on the sofa and jump up on the bed. She loves attention.

My friends, relatives, and coworkers (the former doubters) are all believers now. They remember her birthday and Christmas and always ask about her. They say that Scarlett is a lucky dog. My reply is, "I am the lucky one." I have one friend who told me if she were to die and be reincarnated, she would want to come back to life as Carolyn's dog.

Scarlett has become a loving friend and companion. She has given me joy and helped me through some difficult times during our five years together. Her sweet mood never changes. She has brightened many days and shortened some long nights. She has made me a better person.

To quote the poet William Butler Yeats:

Think where man's glory most begins and ends
And say my glory was I had such friends.

CAROLYN EMERICK

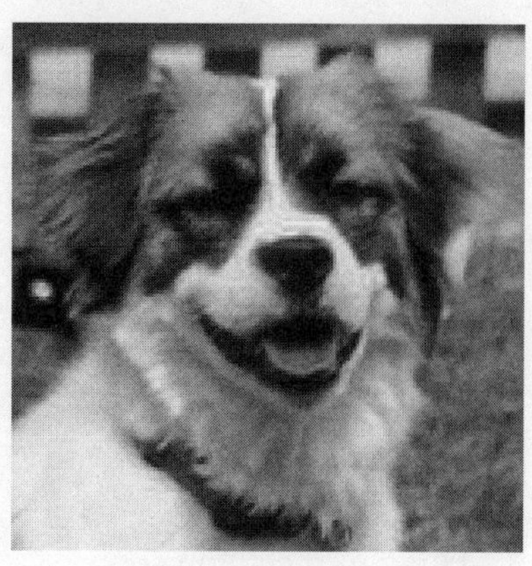

BERNIE
FELCYN-NATALE
("BERNIE")

I am a female Corgi mix who looks like a miniature St. Bernard, hence the name. I am a Humane Society rescue who is looking for someone to play with. Turn-ons are: playing fetch, tug, visiting my friends in the park, and making holes with my big "digger" paws. Turn-offs are: baths, bedtime, being alone in the house, and getting on the scale at the vet.

I hate being alone so much. I won't eat any treats left for me, and I won't play with any of my toys until my parents come home. My favorite thing to do is chew stuff, and I chew a lot when I am bored. Once, when I was left alone in the house, I chewed the wooden magazine rack in my parents' living room. I also chewed up my mom's shoes as well as a towel and the matt in the bathroom. Another time I got bored of my toys and started chewing on my tail. I was able to chew off all of the fur from the tip of my tail.

My favorite treats are peanut butter Kong Stuff'ns, Marro Bones, and compressed rawhide. I do lots of things for those treats, including sit, beg, lay, shake, high-five, speak, growl, and stay. Great places to meet are at PetSmart, the Dog Park, and Daffin Park. At

PetSmart you will find me in the isles barking at other dogs (my favorites are small dogs and puppies) while my mom buys me stuff. At the parks you will find me trying to jump on the biggest dog there. I love to play with dogs bigger than me, especially golden retrievers, because I wish I were a big dog like them.

If your parents have to come with you when we meet, tell them that I love to be pet and scratched. If they do that, I will return the favor with lots of licks, especially on their feet.

Hope to meet you soon,

BERNIE

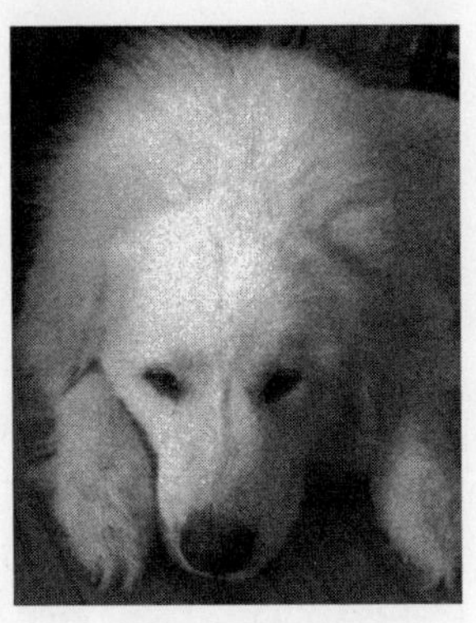

BAILEY

I'm a Pyrenees mountain dog, often referred to as the gentle giant. My owner, Ms. Terri, thinks she rescued me, but actually I am an angel sent to protect her.

When Frederic C. Beil first approached me with the idea of telling my story and having it featured in *Savannah Dogs*, I was thrilled beyond barks. I'm fairly new to Savannah, having moved here on Columbus Day, October 2003, somewhat symbolic, for this journey has truly been a discovery of the life of a dog in Savannah. Knowing the slogan on the early seal of Georgia—Non Sibi, Sed Aliis ("Not for Ourselves, But for Others")—my owner was sure this was a positive sign. I have found that to be true, especially for canines. They could have said, "Not for Ourselves, But for the Dogs." How many places have parties for owners and their canine companions—such as the party that Cora Bett Thomas had on National Bring Your Dog to Work Day? I met my friend Hamilton there, and it was quite a party. Cora Bett supplied the dogs with many amenities, such as scarves, engraved tags, treats, large bowls of water everywhere, and pools to frolic in. For the owners she supplied a wonderful lunch, and they got ball caps. The *Savannah Morning*

News was out to do the story, and I was lucky enough to make it in that story.

Savannah also has a wine bar called Venus de Milo. They invite owners and their canines in for a social. They have plenty of wine for the owners as well as treats and water for the dogs. My owner reached for a treat on the bar and almost ate it herself, but luckily I pawed her quickly enough and was able to retrieve the treat for myself. I think she was thinking they were peanuts. After all, she had never experienced an event like this. I attended this event with Hamilton (standard poodle), Charlie (Tibetan terrier), and Tillie (Aussie), my walking buddies from the Midtown area. My brother Buddie, a Westie, and my friends have started our own walking group. We thought our owners needed more socialization, and we are able to get a little exercise while they have their own little support group going. We all walk about an hour in the morning and thirty minutes at night. I highly recommend this type of activity for all canines and humans. It's a great way to get to know your neighbors. Another fun group we started is our Sunday off-leash play group, where we meet and play.

Another great discovery about Savannah is Forsyth Park. It's a great park to meet other single dogs, and there you will find much diversity in the breeds of both owners and canines. Oh, and they have a great canine drinking fountain as well as a people fountain. I must say, I find Savannah a dog-friendly city, and I'm glad I moved here.

BAILEY

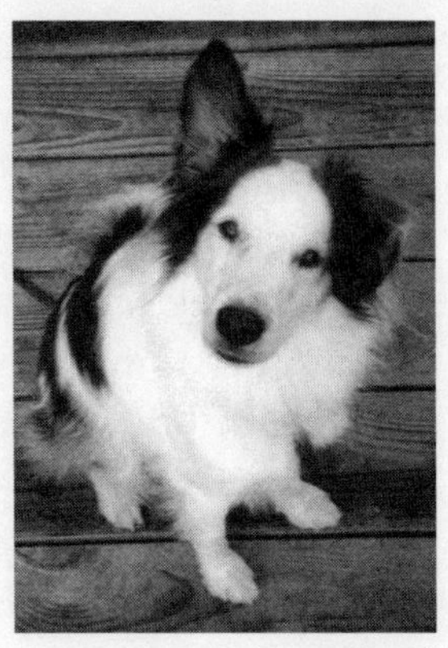

Hamish

As a dog, I don't get many opportunities to tell my story. My earliest memories are of wandering the Georgia countryside. I was abandoned with the rest of my litter, and we became like a pack of wild dogs. I liked roaming around all day, but I knew I was different from the rest of the group. They were mean and often fought with each other, while I just wanted to play. Some farmers started putting out food for us. I thought they were just being nice, but one day they lured us into a truck and drove us to the Humane Society, where some people put us in cages. They named me Andy—what a stupid name!

Pretty soon a lady adopted me, but she left me alone a lot and I dug holes in her garden. When she let me inside, I had "accidents" in the house. After a few days she returned me to the Humane Society. I still can't believe she gave up on me just like that! I thought I'd lost my chance at a good home.

Then I met Matthew and Diane. They were looking for a sweet, mellow dog. Their timing was great, because I was the first one they saw when they walked in the door. They gave me hugs, and I nuzzled in close to them. Matthew said, "He's the one! He's got the snuggle gene!" We have been together ever since. That was two years ago.

Matthew and Diane gave me a new name—Hamish. I've never met another dog with that name. But it beats "Andy." They tell me it's Scottish, given on account of my ancestry. I'm a Shetland sheepdog mix. They have all kinds of other names for me as well. Matthew calls me "Hamie-boy" and "Chumley." Diane calls me "Wee Sausage" and, when I'm bad, "Naughty Monkey."

My coat is silky soft and mostly white, with brown-and-black patches. Some people say I look like Lassie, but I don't know who that is. As you can see from my picture, I have one crazy ear with a mind of its own. Sometimes it sticks straight up, and sometimes it points to the side. I am about knee-high and built for speed. Some dogs have big thick legs, but mine are like little thin sticks. When I play with other dogs, I'm often the fastest in the group. I love it when bigger dogs try to catch up with me. Playing in big parks is my favorite because then I have enough room to run faster than everyone else. At home, though, I'm as quiet as a mouse and I like to sleep a lot.

The only thing I hate about living with Matthew and Diane is all the baths. People always say how clean and pure my white coat looks. If only they knew what I had to endure! And the other dogs make fun of me when I smell like piña colada–scented shampoo. I haven't been able to train them out of that bad habit. But with all the cuddles, walks, and treats they give me, I'll overlook their flaws.

HAMISH

126

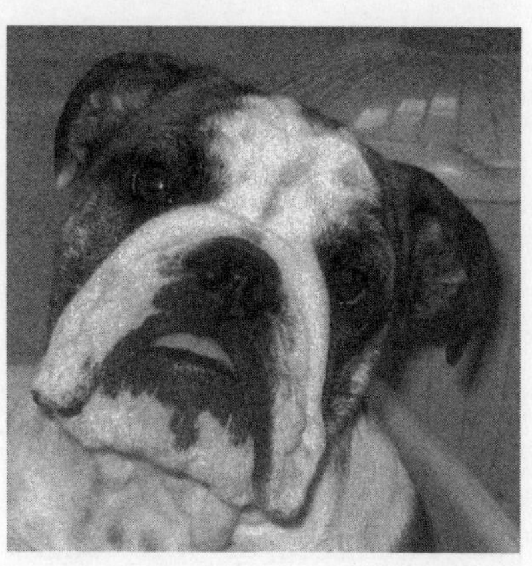

ROXY

On the Road with Roxy . . .

June 12, 2004 . . . on the road

Hi, Journal,

I'm an English bulldog. I bet you're wondering why a dog is on the road. Well, it all started out like this. I needed a camp to go to in the summer, and the only one open was a dog circus camp, so I signed up. Little did I know it was a travel camp that lasted the whole summer, so you had to sleep on a bus until the summer was over and they had to bring you back before school started. So, I'm traveling to Atlanta, Georgia, for our first show.

June 24, 2004 . . . making progress

I can't say we didn't make any progress because we did before our next show. Ozzie, a Great Dane, finally learned how to juggle poodles. Ting, a Pekingese [see pages 129–30], learned how to fit into a toy elephant costume half her size, and Rita, a Chihuahua, learned how to eat twenty hot dogs in less than a minute! I learned my act, which was the cannonball shoot, in the first week. It was cool. The trapeze was my favorite part even though they said I was too overweight. I still wanted to try it, so I did. And let's just say being stuck upside down in the middle of the night for hours was not fun.

July 4, 2004 . . . after the show

Our first show was a big hit. The crowd went crazy! After the show, we had fireworks and we all talked about how fun it was. Then we all went into our rooms and fell asleep. In the middle of the night I got up to use the bathroom and walked by the pugs' room and saw them standing on top of each other putting up a sign that read: "Notice: This is our room, not yours, so do not enter!" They say pugs are the smartest animals! Ha.

July 28 and 29, 2004 . . . shows

The next two days we did five big shows in Tennessee, Mississippi, Florida, New York, and Colorado. We didn't have any trouble going to sleep the two nights, even though we were on a bus.

August 1, 2004 . . . home sweet home

Today summer will be over and I will be home. I know my mother missed me because she called me every day to see if the food was okay and wanted to know if she needed to send anything extra. I can't believe I'm saying this, but I think I will sign up next year too!

ROXY

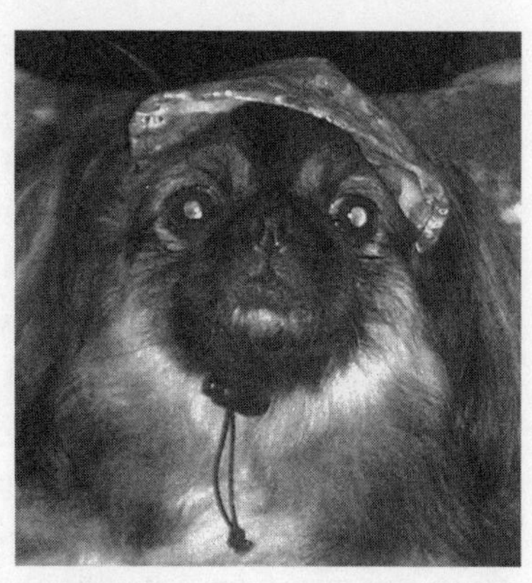

TING

It's all about me, me, me . . . Ting!

About five years ago, I found the great home after being lost on the street. I was sick with heartworms. The Gordon family took me in and took me to Dr. Bink, who made me well. Now I have the most perfect little girl to be my best friend. Her name is Kenerly. I have other friends too. There are lots of outside farm animals, including four big dogs, but I don't get to play with them too much. I'm inside with my other best friends: Rita, the Chihuahua, and Missy Kitty, a calico cat. Rita and I play all day, running circles around the furniture. Sometimes Missy plays too. She even arches her back to play "scary kitty" some days.

When Rita gets tired and wants to nap (she's older and does that a lot), I have all my squeaky toys and bones to keep me busy. I even have my own toy box with my name on it, just so everyone knows whose toys those are.

What keeps me busiest is running after Kenerly when she is home from school. I have to make every step she does. I don't miss a thing. When she has friends over, it can be really rough with all those girls. We may play dress-up or Polly Pockets (I like to hide those little pieces), or on some days we play restaurant. I like those days the best because I can eat anything the girls drop, if Rita doesn't get it first.

Dress-up is not so bad either. I have my own cap, scarf, and matching collar and leash. I have a great T-shirt that says "Yuppie Puppy." Not what a typical farm dog would wear, but I'm special. I got to walk in the Guyton Christmas Parade with my neighbor Roxy, the English bulldog. (You might have heard about me in her story [see pages 127–28]. We went to circus camp this summer, sort of anyway!)

Yeah. I'm always busy around here. Buddy (the min-macaw), Lacy (the cockatiel), and the parakeets make so much noise during the day that I can't nap much, even when Kenerly is at school. I shouldn't complain. After all, I have a huge bed in Kenerly's room, plus my own stool so I can jump up into bed with her when I want. Missy Kitty gets to sleep on the other twin bed, and sometimes with us.

Speaking of . . . gotta go! Kenerly just grabbed her stuffed bunny to head upstairs. It must be bedtime. Gotta find my stuffed bunny and run up there too. I'll sit in the bathroom and play with my squeaky bunny for a few minutes while she brushes her teeth. Then I'm off to bed for a Milk-Bone snack and to go night-night. Tomorrow will be another busy day.

TING

130

HARLEY

That big stick is coming down on my tiny back, again! And my human is so big, so angry, that I can never run fast enough to be safe from his wrath.

The pain is so deep—so strong that I can only hope he will fall asleep for a very long time. Sleep is the safe time of my days and nights. His, not mine.

I always want to please my human, but I have no doggoned idea what he wants from me. He will throw the ball—though he almost always throws it at me, not to me—which makes it very difficult for a dog of my size to enjoy one of the important feats of life, playing.

The sound of freedom, or so I thought, came when the doorbell rang one day and interrupted my human's wrath with the cane. It was the nice, old lady next door asking my human to please let her take me somewhere so he could have a quieter life. She talked a long time and in the end of the loudness picked me up, walked to her car, and drove me to the Humane Society Animal Shelter.

Now I've gone from pain, to impending death.

No one wanted a mottled, filthy, little mongrel such as me, for everyone wanted cute. I heard a human say, "Oh, look at him. He is absolutely precious. Do you want to go home with me, little Fluffy?"

Well, I thought my heart would burst wide open when I heard this woman's soft voice, and I licked her fingers through the prison bars.

Happiness was just around the comer—that is, after that one horrible stop my new mommy had to make with me. She was getting me neutered. Ouch!

I got over my anger pretty quickly as she picked me up, and without worrying one bit about my dirty little body, placed me in her brand new car.

She loves me. I love her.

I have a very large sofa, a leather chair with matching ottoman, a gigantic bed loaded with lots of soft pillows, and a down comforter. My mommy says I'm spoiled because I will only lie on soft things. This is true. After all, she has a soft heart for me, as well as my human daddy, so all I know is soft love. My name is now Harley.

HARLEY

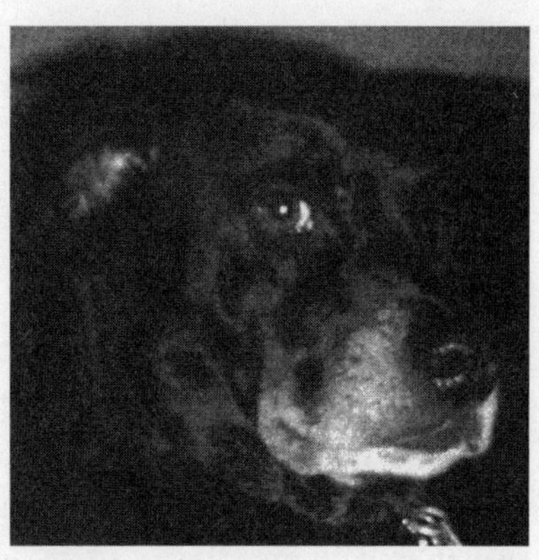

ABLE

I'm certainly Able! It was in June that my world was turned upside down. I was taken from my owners, whom I loved despite their abuse, and within the space of a week I was unabatedly placed in a shelter where my liberties were stripped, self-esteem plunged, and health was even accosted.

While I was at least no longer being physically abused, my state of affairs was in dire need of change. I grew thinner as my weight went down, and was not allowed proper amounts of exercise required for the treatment of my broken leg, which was contracted about two years prior to these events—another story to be told on another day. I needed a home, but was unable to find one for myself, let alone the dignity of any space to call my own. For that matter, I was barely able to maintain any sense of dignity at all, but if I am anything, I am Able.

See, that's my name and has been even before Mark found me. He's my new owner, and he likes to think that my name's not so much a biblical one as that it is meant to be related to my ability. He enjoys that I am an example of a principle he personally heavily believes

in—that of rehabilitation. For Mark and me, rehabil-
itation really refers to any animal's personal will to
overcome the things that plague them and to reclaim a
rightful happiness. I think he wants me to be an exam-
ple of that, and I am certainly doing my best! Since
Mark took me in, my attitude has improved, and not
only am I starting to allow my true qualities (devotion,
friendliness, and affection) to show through, but Mark
has learned valuable lessons as well. He seems to
understand that with privilege comes responsibility,
and that it is his charge to take care of me. I think he
does a good job, and I am happy enough that it shows
when my picture is taken.

ABLE

Sophie

Sophie was bom in Blackville, South Carolina, on July 15, 1989. She was the runt of the litter and the last to leave. In her first week with us she cried every night and almost had to be returned to her country home. Things got better, however, and soon Sophie became very comfortable with her new family.

She was the easiest dog to train that we had ever experienced. She was house-trained in a couple of weeks. She had a natural fetching instinct and without any training was fetching balls and toys. She even had a natural ability to catch small toys out of the air. Sophie has a strong urge to please her family and has never needed any more discipline than a harsh word. In fact, when the father of the family got upset at her and showed strong emotion through a raised voice, Sophie would wet the floor. As a result the discipline was soon turned over to Sophie's mother.

Sophie has always loved family activities and likes to get in the middle of any family hugs. She would find a way to participate in many games with our son when he was young. One of her favorite games was hallway bowling. Our son would roll a small plastic bowling ball down a long hall toward a small set of hard plastic pins. Our son's goal was to knock down all the pins while Sophie's was to catch the ball before it hit any pins. Zack and Sophie could play this game for hours.

Our son's favorite Sophie story is when her cousin Millie, a full-sized Airedale, came for a visit. Sophie had never been around such a big dog, and after Millie came into our house, Sophie immediately began running away. As Millie got closer, Sophie quickened her pace, but Millie was closing in (with tail wagging). This was too much for Sophie, however, and she began dropping little brown obstacles in Millie's way. This resulted in Sophie's immediate removal to the backyard, a safe distance away. Our son says he was able to learn very early on what it meant to have "the crap scared out of you."

Sophie learned English very well (again without intentional training), and soon we were having to spell words that would get her too excited. Bedtime was Sophie's favorite time of day; and when this was announced (unless it was spelled), Sophie would grab the nearest toy in sight, growl and bark with it in her mouth, and run around frantically (with tail wagging) until Zack and parents were safely upstairs.

Sophie patiently endured considerable teasing and harassment from Zack and only one time bore her teeth and went after him. One morning, after more than a tolerable amount of deviling-up, Sophie bore her teeth, growled, and chased after Zack, who turned tail and received a nip in the right buttock. He went running to his mother to complain of the attack, but could only produce a slightly red spot, and was simply told this served him right. This did little to interfere with the growing bond between the two. In fact later, at his first day of pre-kindergarten, Zack and his classmates were all asked to talk about their families. When it came to Zack's turn, he reported that he had no brothers and one sister, but she was a dog.

One of Sophie's favorite times has always been her birthday and Christmas. She opens her wrapped gifts with enthusiasm and then works feverishly to chew out the squeakers contained in each. She never tired of her toys and by the end of each day could always be counted on to have removed each one from her toy bin until she had distributed all of them throughout the house.

One birthday, we took her through the drive-thru window at Dairy Queen, and the cashier was so surprised to see a canine customer that he gave her a free kid-sized ice cream cone. What a big day that was! Sophie smiled all the way home.

As with many dogs, Sophie loves to ride in the car with her head out the window. Unlike some dogs, if she is not held tightly she would easily fall out!

Sophie loves being close to her mom so much, she follows her everywhere. One night, while her mom was having a nice, relaxing soak, Sophie jumped into the bathtub to join in on the fun.

These days Sophie doesn't move quite as quickly as she did in her youth. She is content to sit in the passenger seat on car trips and waits to be carried up and down the steps to the yard so she can "do her business." According to her vet, Dr. Bink, for a fifteen-year-old Sophie's in good shape. She still likes to be near the action of her family even if she's napping. She has been the best dog ever and a joy to have around.

She has even been chosen the favorite granddog of the many granddogs in our larger family.

Sophie's been a wonderful addition to our little family, and she will forever live in our hearts.

LOU AND ALISON IMBROGNO

Bear Creek's Kokomo Sunset ("Kokomo")

Hello, Friends! I am an Army Brat that was born in Montana and has spent the past five years of my life constantly moving from one state to another. I have lived in El Paso, Texas; Lawton, Oklahoma; Starkville, Mississippi; and now Savannah, Georgia.

I am a typical spoiled Lab that "owns" my house and has earned the highly coveted "Couch Potato" distinction. Most of my friends instantly notice my larger than normal tongue. The good Lord blessed me with a large tongue so I can give my friends and family an enormous amount of love and affection. (Ears are my favorite!) I enjoy nothing more than playing games; swimming; chasing tree frogs, cats, and squirrels; playing in mud holes; and of course at the end of the day, lying belly-up on the couch. If I get bored, I can invent a game out of just about anything from my football to a dirty sock. I am versatile, and I am always ready no matter what comes my way.

As I previously stated, I am an Army Brat. My parents are dual-military, so I get to spend lots of time with my grandparents in Starkville. My first duty station was Fort Bliss, Texas. While I was not a fan of the sand, I was a huge fan of all the hiking and camping places in New Mexico and Colorado. While in Texas, my parents got deployed and my sister (Buffett, a yellow lab) and I got to spend nine months with our grandparents. Pop and Gram were incredibly good to us and often spoiled us with extra snacks. My next duty station was Fort Sill, Oklahoma. We were only stationed here for eight months; I became, however, a huge fan of the Wildlife Refuge. I got to run, swim, hike, and camp and just enjoy the outdoors. Weekends were always a welcome site in Oklahoma.

In September 2002 my parents moved to Fort Stewart, Georgia. We were only here a short while be-fore both of my parents left for Iraq. Buffett and I got to go live with our grandparents again. While I love Pop and Gram very much, this deployment was much harder than the first. Pop, Gram, Buffett, and I sent care packages and wrote doggie letters just about every week. Then one day in August 2003 Pop and Gram took Buffett and me for a long car ride from Mississippi to Fort Stewart. We sat by bleachers on a parade field for a few hours with lots of crazy humans yelling, screaming, and waving banners and flags. Buffett and I had no idea what was going on until we heard our parents yelling our names. My heart was complete again!

During this past year some of my favorite pastimes have been swimming in the ocean at Tybee Island, walking around on River Street, hanging out in City

Market, eating pizza at Vinnie's, and lying under a table in front of Six Pence people watching.

It is rough having both parents serving our country during these times; I am, however, just fortunate to have the love and support of awesome grandparents. I am always ready for whatever the future holds!

KOKOMO

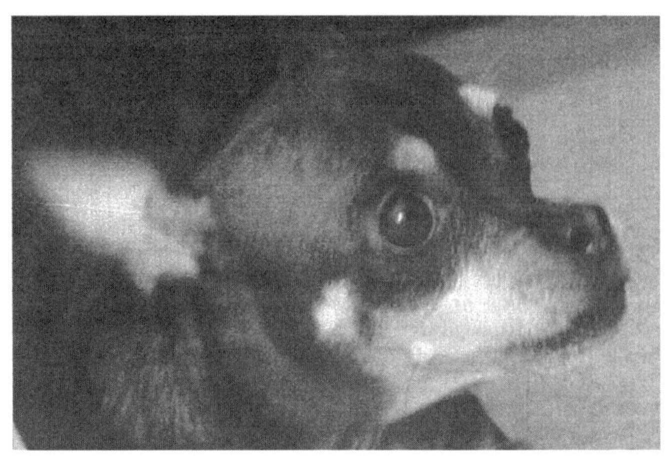

LITTLE BIT OF PRECIOUS II JARRIEL ("LITTLE BIT")

Hi, my name actually started out "Little Bit of Precious," but when my mommy and daddy registered me with the AKC, "II" was added. (Imagine, two of me!) I am called Little Bit because I am a Chihuahua. I am eight years old and the apple of my mommy and daddy's eye. I have a three-year-old brother named Ashton, but he isn't a dog. He's a cat. (I think he was adopted!) I must say, he is quite annoying. He likes to chew on my legs like drumsticks, and I don't like that too much. I do like to take car rides and go camping. I also like to visit with Papa and Nana (because my Nana likes to sneak me treats). I probably shouldn't say that because my vet, Dr. Christopher Gall, tells my mommy and daddy that I shouldn't have too many treats, but you know how Nanas are! My daddy's sister, Kay, likes to feed me too.

I don't care too much about going to the local pet store though. I get nervous around other dogs. Do you want to hear a really funny story? When my mommy and daddy brought me home for the first time, they took me to this famous pet store in Savannah to buy me a pretty hot-pink harness and leash. Well, after they picked it out and tried it on me, they let me wear it while we were walking in the store. When we got to the end of an aisle, there sat a very, very large St. Bernard. You need to know that I only weighed one and a half pounds. Well, I took one look at him and promptly backed myself out of my pretty hot pink harness and ran up into my mommy's shorts. That caused quite a lot of hollering and laughter from everyone around. My daddy really thought it was funny because I was so little that he couldn't "find me," and my mommy kept hollering to get me out! I finally came out alright, but I wasn't going near that St. Bernard. So my daddy held me for the rest of that trip. I don't like to go back there. You never know when a St. Bernard might be waiting for you! I like it, how-ever, when my mommy and daddy go because they bring me back t-r-e-a-t-s. (Don't tell Mommy and Daddy, but I can spell!)

We live out in the country. I had to get used to the country life because we used to live in town. One of the best things about being a country dog is all of the open space. My backyard is much bigger than my old one. I am quite small compared to the other country dogs. So I like to go outside and get all of the other dogs barking and howling, and then I go inside and listen to my "neighbors" chit-chat.

I hope you enjoyed getting to read a little bit about me, and be sure to give the dog in your life a scratch behind the ears!

LITTLE BIT

BRANDON JONES ("MR. B")

I am an eleven-year-old Afghan hound from Georgia's first city, Savannah. My rich natural beauty enthralls most people. I think that alone makes me a Savannah dog. My coat is covered with long silky hair that requires hours of grooming each week in order to maintain its beautiful appearance. Most people often consider me a show dog when they see me for the first time. My dad always corrects them by telling them that I am an Afghan hound and not a show dog.

It is funny how people always want to touch and pet me. They are not aware that I am a bit standoffish and shy when I first meet strangers. Nor do I enjoy being petted on the head. How would they feel if strangers greeted them with a pat on the head? I enjoy running free. My dad seems to think that because I am aloof I should be on a leash or in a fenced area under his supervision at all times when I am outside. I am also a sight hound, which means that if something gets my attention I will take off after it without thought of running in front of a moving vehicle. I love chasing cats and squirrels about as much as I love walking through the parks here in Savannah. It is in my nature to chase after anything small that seems to be moving. I really enjoy Savannah.

Savannah is the most beautiful city that I have ever seen, and believe me, I have been to some nice cities. My dad adopted me from the Chatham–Savannah Humane Society when I was six months old. Life has been great ever since the day my dad took me to my new home. My dad introduced me to the good life. He usually brings breakfast, lunch, and dinner to my bedside. He takes me on walks after each meal. Seems like I have done a great job at training him. After my weekly grooming appointment, my dad and I usually take a stroll through the Historic District and downtown Savannah. My dad says that is my treat for being good at the groomers, but I think that is his way of showing off his handsome son to the many tourists and locals that are out and about. The walks with my dad make me proud to be a Savannah dog.

My other favorite city in Georgia has to be Cordele. My grandmother lives in Cordele, and when I go to visit her she really spoils me. Grandmothers are really great to have around because when my dad says "no" my Grandma Ruby usually says "yes."

I had a sister that stayed with my grandmother after my dad left for college. Unfortunately Sheba has gone on to doggy heaven. Sheba was fourteen years old when her health started to fail, and she had to be put to sleep. Sheba and I had loads of fun together, and I really do miss her. If Sheba were still around, she would ask my dad to help her write a story. She often visited Savannah and would have considered herself a Savannah dog as well.

To all you non-Savannah dogs and parents, I would like to encourage you all to really consider visiting

Savannah. You will be captivated by Savannah's gracious charm and natural beauty. The serene landscape, squares, and parks in the Historic District would make you want to become a Savannah dog or parent. Most of our visitors enjoy the quaint atmosphere of the cobblestone waterfront (River Street) lined with many unique shops and restaurants. They often call my dad and tell him how much they enjoyed their stay and can't wait until they get a chance to come back. That is why I love being a Savannah dog.

BRANDON

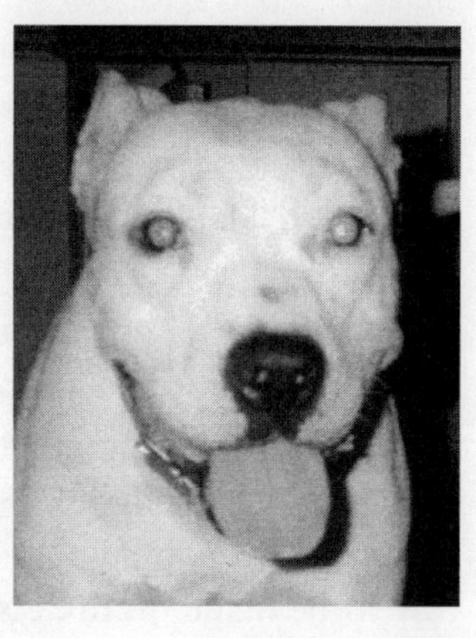

Big Mamma
("Mamma")

I truly believe that my first tumultuous encounter with Big Mamma was an act of divine intervention. It had to have been because I cannot come up with any other explanation as to why my mother and I stopped at the Chatham County Animal Control Shelter on that hot July afternoon over a year ago. Something caused us to stop and see what kinds of dogs were being kept there. And that's when she got me. Oh, no, it was not love at first sight or anything of that warm, fuzzy nature. When I first saw her, my heart broke. She and her small puppy were the saddest, most neglected dogs I had ever seen. Every bone in Mamma's body was visible, she had open sores and scabs all over, her nails were so long that they bent her feet against the concrete floor, and the amount of filth and dirt that was caked on her white fur was unimaginable.

Her little puppy, whom I called Bambino, was not in much better shape. His belly looked like it was going to explode because he had so many worms. One of the workers informed us that the previous owners had moved and left the dogs locked up for weeks with no

147

food or water, and that was how they ended up in the shelter. Nothing else was known of their past.

Needless to say, my heart went out to them, and I wanted to help them immediately. Unfortunately, because they were a cruelty case, Mamma and Bambino were being held there until the owners were caught and prosecuted. The police officer had no leads and no possible way to find them. And so began my daily visits to the shelter. For over a month I brought Mamma and Bambino food and treats as I waited for progress to be made on the case. The case was at a standstill when finally, in the middle of August, it became apparent that I could no longer wait. Both dogs' health was deteriorating. Bambino had stopped eating and was so weak he could barely open his eyes; and Mamma, a full-grown pit bull, only weighed twenty pounds, and that was after a month's work of fattening her up.

After I called the police officer and explained the crucial situation, he released both dogs to me. We left the shelter and headed straight for the vet, where I got very disheartening news. Little Bambino, who had barely even had a chance at life, was in bad shape and there was nothing that could be done for him. There was slightly better news for Big Mamma. She had every parasite and worm possible, including heartworms, but she would be able to pull through with immediate intervention. I brought them home, and ignoring what the vet said, tried to "rescue" Bambino. It did not work. He passed the same night I had finally got him out of the shelter and into my home. As devastated as I was, I had to be thankful that he was even able to experience some love and kindness in his short life. After Bambino passed, I was determined that Big Mamma was not going to suffer the same sad fate.

I got in contact with a wonderful organization on the Internet, Pit Bull Rescue Central (www.pbrc.net), and with their complete financial support I was able to get Big Mamma completely healthy. And at sixty-plus pounds she is living up to her name. She has been such a wonderful addition to my life that I don't know how I made it without her before.

Now it has not been a complete fairy tale. We have experienced a lot of prejudice and ignorance because of the fact that she is a pit bull, and that breed has tons of media hype and myths surrounding it. If, however, there ever was a pit bull to prove those myths wrong, it's Mamma! Pit bulls are portrayed as fiercely aggressive dogs, which can "snap" at any moment and ravage anything in its path. Well, let me tell you about my "fierce" pit bull. The only thing that should cower in fear of being torn to shreds by Mamma is the stuffed squeaky toy in her toy box. When I pull out my vacuum cleaner, my "fearless fighter" runs and hides under the bed. When we come across a stranger on our walks, my "insatiably aggressive" canine strains at her leash, so that she might get the chance to greet the stranger with slobbery kisses and dirty paws. And I am no pet psychic, but I can almost guarantee that anytime she sees another dog, she is thinking "Oh, goody, goody, a new best friend for me to play with!" So Big Mamma has survived her cruel and unimaginable past, and has triumphantly gone on to spread her wonderful pit-bull loving to anyone who crosses her path!

SARAH JORDAN

Max

I was born on September 16, 1996. It was a very lucky day for me when my dad purchased me as a Christmas gift for my mommy on December 16, 1996. And I must say, life has been totally awesome since then!

I'm a Peek-a-Poo, and my mommy says I got the best qualities of both breeds. My hair is wavy (not poodle curly) and extremely soft. And the best part about my hair is that I don't shed. Because I'm such a loving, loyal, and cute companion, my parents pamper me to quite the extreme. For example, I have my own room, affectionately referred to as "the condo." It is fully equipped with everything a fine pooch like myself could ever want—food and water, nice cushy bed, a radio that plays twenty-four hours a day, seven days a week, for my entertainment. And there are two windows that allow me to look outside during the day when my mom and dad are working. My room even has a sign on the front door that let's everyone know this is "Max's Room."

I am involved in many activities, including, but not limited to, taking long walks with my mom, riding in the car anywhere, but especially to my grandpa's house on Saturday mornings, playing indoor soccer with my "big ball" for hours at a time, wrestling with socks and towels, and occasionally trying to start up a game of "let's play" with my sister Spooky. Unfortunately, because she is a cat, she is not quite as enthusiastic about playing as I am. And when it comes to jumping, my mom says I could have been in the circus. Just put a toy or treat in front of me, and I can jump as high as you want me to!

Not only am I beloved by my parents, I have several extended family members who also love me very much. When my parents take a vacation, I get a vacation too, at my Aunt Susie's house. Along with Uncle Pete and cousins Ryan and Katie, Aunt Susie provides me with lots of tender-loving care while I'm at her house. Also, my Aunt Barbara and my Aunt Kelly spoil me at Christmas time with gifts and treats. Oh, and I can't forget about my Mimi and Papa's house, where it's nice and quiet. I really enjoy staying there sometimes, too. Papa loves to be sneaky and give me treats that I shouldn't have when Mommy is not looking.

So as you can see, I am quite spoiled, but it is well deserved as I am a good boy and mind all adults very well. My mom is totally in love with me, and my dad thinks I'm pretty great too! If you ever have the chance to bring home a new puppy, my parents would advise you to do so.

MAX

It was a typical late January day—wet, overcast, and cold—one of those short January days that cause you to relish the heat of August. As my workdays were spent outside, I took little joy in my daily tasks during those short winter months. So imagine my surprise when I returned to my office and found a teeny-tiny puppy lying on a blanket under my desk. The puppy was maybe four to five weeks old, her eyes were barely open, and what you could see through the tiny slits was a blue-gray color. Her coat was in horrible condition, covered with dirt, mud, and open wounds. It turns out that a customer of mine, knowing of my love for dogs, brought this horrific-looking little creature to me to nurture back to some semblance of life. According to the customer, he had found three puppies in the Dempsey Dumpster at Thirty-eighth and Habersham streets. He kept one, I received the second, and the third little puppy did not make it.

At that time I owned a rather large black Lab named Simba [see *Savannah Dogs II*, pages 254–58], who weighed in at 122 pounds. Adding another dog to the mix was dicey at best, yet raising a puppy of unknown origin was a long reach even for an avid dog lover. The other unknown was how my beautiful wife would respond to the puppy. Oh, she loves dogs too, but she is also allergic to their hair and dander.

Of course I am getting the cart in front of the horse here as this pathetic little creature was in extremely poor health and had been residing inside a garbage receptacle for who knows how long. What exactly was wrong with her and what was it going to take to make her healthy again? I know that this may sound cynical to some, but as much as we love dogs we cannot take in every stray that passes our way. Fortunately my innate affection for the puppy won out over my deep-seated fears of the unknown. That evening I wrapped up the little puppy in a blanket and carried her home. Both Simba and my lovely bride rejected my new little girl. Simba, because he had no desire to share the roost; my bride, because she had no desire to raise a new puppy. After a fretful night for all concerned (Simba paced the floor all night), I carried my little bundle of joy to my favorite veterinarian the following morning and left her in his care. Several hours later his office called to advise that in addition to several types of worms, ear mites, scabies, and numerous wounds, my newest best friend would, in all likelihood, survive to see another day. That was good news for the puppy and myself, but the rest of my household was not too thrilled.

I picked up my friend after work and tried to formulate my words of explanation to both my wife and Simba. We were living on Tattnall and Charleton streets at the time in a beautiful two-story home. I did not want to just waltz into the house with the puppy in her blanket, so I opened my shirt and tucked her inside. With my jacket on, you could not see the bulge. Once inside it took Simba all of two seconds to realize I had the puppy with me. Simba's whining alerted my wife that something was amiss; it was all downhill from there. I prepared a box in the TV room upstairs for the puppy, which did not go well with Simba at all. From Simba's perspective, too much attention was being paid to the newcomer. My wife just shook her head and announced that she was not cleaning up after the puppy.

Everyone involved survived the first night home. All accidents were cleaned up; and as I headed off to work with Simba in tow, I placed the puppy back inside of my shirt. It was warm and comfy, and it allowed me to drive without worrying about the puppy. Simba was ignoring me and the puppy, but that was to be expected. Once at the office, a new box was created and my little friend was stashed in the back office for safekeeping. The day progressed without incident, aside from Simba barking at the puppy on one or two occasions. At the close of business it was back inside my shirt and back to the house. It was still January and still wet and cold outside, no suitable conditions for a small puppy. This scenario played out for several days, and everyone was adjusting reasonably well to the new addition.

We still had not named our new friend, but nothing had occurred or come to mind that would trigger a good idea for a name. The night we cooked out on the grill and let the puppy out on the deck. Her eyes were open now, and she was moving around as best she could, given her age. After dinner I gave Simba some scraps of meat and watched in amazement as he walked away from the steak. Was he really that upset about the puppy? I left the meat out, knowing full well that he would devour it as soon as I turned my head. As I checked the house before retiring for the night, I found the steak scraps right where I left them. Very strange.

The puppy was very active that night, and Simba was heard roaming the wood floors, with his nails, clickety-clack, all night long. No one slept very well, and Simba, not at all. I was truly concerned about Simba when I entered the kitchen that morning and the steak was still in his bowl.

My concern grew considerably when we went to get into the truck and Simba collapsed trying to hop up in the cab! Once at the office and everything was settled, I carried Simba to the vet and left him. I feared the worst and did not have the heart to hang around to hear what the vet had to say. Simba was around nine years old, but certainly had not been showing any signs of diminished capacity. Sure, he did not chase the squirrels with the same passion as before, but he still gave the tree rats a good run for their money. Around two o'clock the vet called to advise that Simba had cancer and several large masses within the stomach.

Through my tears I quizzed the Doc about treatment and the quality of life for Simba. I could hear the Doc shaking his head through the phone. I asked him to put Simba down for me as I could not bear to look into those big ol' eyes of his one last time. I picked Simba up later that evening and buried him next to his ol' friend Amoco [see *Savannah Dogs*, pages 296–98]. Why does it hurt so bad and so deep? If there is a doggie heaven, I feel confident they both made it.

After breaking the news to my wife that evening, we discussed the why and the how of things and came to the conclusion that an angel must have sent the puppy to us, knowing that Simba was not long for this world. We now had a name for the puppy, Gabrielle. She is now around two years old and is a beautiful chocolate Lab whom we call Gabby. She cannot replace Simba, but she has more than filled the void.

BROTHER LOGAN

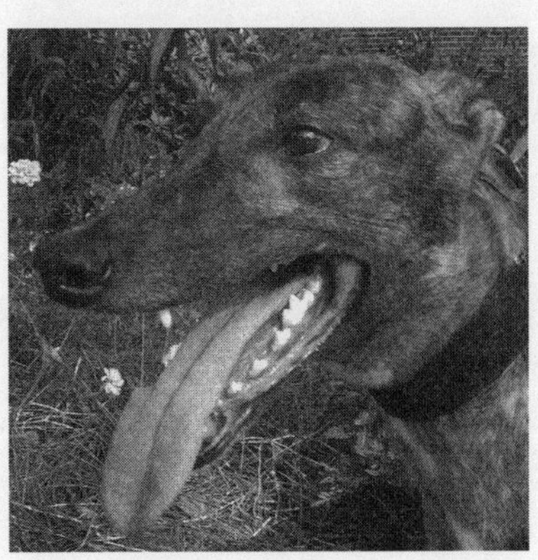

I have been in love with greyhounds ever since I adopted Max, a three-and-a-half-year-old male. They are such a charming breed, combining elegance and grace with total goofiness. They are wonderful house pets, needing far less exercise that most people think, and are perfectly content to flop on the couch all day if allowed. Greyhounds are generally nonaggressive and get along well with other dogs. They like children once they learn about them, and many coexist quite happily with house cats, after being properly introduced.

I am a member of the Savannah Friends of Greyhounds as Pets (SFGAP), a group dedicated to educating people about greyhounds. They lend their support to Greyhounds as Pets of Northeast Florida, who run the adoption center at the Jacksonville Dog Track, and they participate in the Greyhound Underground Railroad, where volunteer drivers from Florida up as far as Ohio and Delaware transport groups of "greys" to waiting families, passing them along like so many furry batons in a relay race. SFGAP also responds to the pleas that come over the Internet from various rescue groups on behalf of dogs in desperate situations. They hold fund-raisers and take donations to help offset the medical bills that these dogs can generate and to make it easier for families to provide homes. It was one of these Internet pleas that got to me last year.

The message described five brood dogs that were going to be put down if homes were not found by the coming weekend. Since I was already a three-dog household, I reminded myself over and over that I didn't need any more. Still I found myself checking the computer each night and saw with relief that one by one the dogs were spoken for. On Thursday night, however, one last dog remained and the plea went out again, "Please, please, will someone adopt this dog?" I decided that a house with three dogs could make room for one more, and I picked up the phone.

I was told that she would be arriving in Savannah on a truck hauling dogs to various locations around the country and that I would get a phone call telling me when and where to pick her up. Sure enough, at 5:00 A.M. on Saturday the call came and I scrambled to the rendezvous at the I-95 and 204 exit. When I got out of the car, the driver gave me some paperwork and thrust a leash into my hand. I looked down at a skinny, terrified, dark brindle female with a large bruise on her abdomen. She had been shaved, had numerous sores and abscesses all over her body, and rotten teeth. I fell instantly in love. She was beautiful!

Adopting a greyhound is always an adventure. Like most of them, my new girl had never been in a house, so everything—stairs, carpeting, windows, even other breeds of dogs—were new and, as far as she was concerned, frightening. When I brought her into the living room, she stood panting, eyes wide and darting all around. Then she saw Max. The relief at finding something familiar was evident as she slowly walked up to him and tucked her head under his neck. She didn't realize it yet, but she was home.

I named her Sweet Pea, because she has such a sweet nature. I took her to the vet that same morning. Because greyhounds are used to being handled from birth throughout their time at the racetrack, they are usually very calm and accepting of human attention. Sweet Pea submitted to all the vet's ministrations without complaint, and we emerged later with a bag full of medications, shampoos, and lotions. She also needed dental attention, so more appointments were set up for a cleaning and to pull the teeth that were too rotten to save. I am happy to say that now, a year later, Sweet Pea has a shiny coat, a happy smile, and she looks as beautiful on the outside as she is on the inside.

Her true personality has surfaced, too. It is so much fun to see a greyhound learn to let their "inner dog" out. Because they have had such a regimented lifestyle, they often don't stop to smell the roses, so to speak, and regard things like doggie toys with disinterest or puzzlement. Sweet Pea has always been a joy to walk on a leash, moving when I move and stopping when I stop, never pulling ahead or taking detours. But she also kept her head down and didn't take much notice of her surroundings. Now she still has nice leash manners, but she also checks out the interesting sites and smells around her. She has never warmed up to the dog toys, though, and is happy to leave them to our other furry family members.

I found out through Internet searches that Sweet Pea was a Champion Grade A and had raced for five years, which is considered to be the maximum. Then she had been retired to a brood farm, where she gave birth to nineteen puppies. When she became too old to breed, the call was put out to save her life. Thousands of greyhounds are destroyed each year as their racing careers or breeding usefulness ends, and thousands more are born each year as owners try for that champion dog. Fortunately, more and more rescue groups and concerned animal lovers are helping to find homes for them; and more and more racetracks, like the one in Jacksonville, Florida, are embracing a "no kill" policy and actively supporting adoption. And every adoption counts, believe me. We can make a difference, dog by dog. I have made a difference in Sweet Pea's life, and she has surely made a difference in mine.

If you are interested in finding out more about greyhounds please visit:

www.geocities.com/savannagrey .

KATHLEEN JORDAN AND MARLAINE KIRTON

ROSIE LEE LOVE ("ROSIE")

Rosie Lee Love is my best friend and playmate. Rosie is a "borderline collie" mix. She has very soft and shiny hair and a wonderful personality (kind, gentle, quiet, calm, and settled).

Children love Rosie and she loves them very much. When we had to evacuate for Hurricane Floyd, Rosie went with us. She helped me feel calm and happy. Rosie likes to just "hang out." We take her to the dirty-dog dip as often as we can. She has been to the Roundhouse, and to Daffin and Forsyth parks to support fund-raisers.

Stephanie Hazlett is Rosie's vet and takes wonderful care of her. Rosie had to have serious knee surgery, and Dr. Hazlett took extraspecial care of her and made sure that she had the best care available.

I am very lucky to have Rosie for a pet. I love my dog very much. Thank you for letting me tell you about my dog.

REBEKAH LOVE

Poko

His name was originally Coco, then Rocco, and now Poko. He's had a rough year, this spotted dog. Last September his people gave him to the ASPCA, but within a few weeks Willing Hearts Dalmatian Rescue had found a foster home for him. About the same time, I was looking for a Dalmatian on Petfinder.com. You see, I'd had another Dalmatian, and after he died, six years ago, I didn't think I'd ever be able to have another dog. I was afraid I was a one-dog woman, but I was willing to try. Petfinder is like a dating service for canines, felines, and an assorted variety of other pets. They give you a brief bio of the pet and indicate if it is cat, child, and dog friendly—I needed all three. We have four cats, and you can't have a dog with spots that doesn't like children because kids will run up and pet your dog, no matter what their parents have told them. "Pongo! Perdy! You have 101 Dalmatians!" Spotted dogs come with children hanging onto their tails.

Poko's (or rather Rocco's) picture on the Internet didn't do him justice. He looked pitifully frightened and abandoned, but after looking at dogs from Virginia to Ohio, I finally decided to e-mail his foster people. They sent a picture of him on the couch with a New York Giants cap on—I was smitten.

So, on October 31, our thirteenth anniversary, my partner and I went to meet him. He was pretty nervous and looked thin and a bit depressed. And we had a long drive ahead of us—four hours—and I didn't want to have to bring him back if it didn't work out. I wanted to be sure, but how can one really know?

I sat down on the ground and asked him. "I know you've been through a lot in the past two months, and that you're a one-man or one-woman dog, but we're willing to open our hearts and our home to you, if you'll have us. Do you think you can open your heart to us?" A quick dab of the tongue told me what his tail could not. On the way home our new dog crawled into my lap and fell asleep with his head against my chest, and I felt a hole in my heart close that had been gaping open with unresolved grief for the past six years. I missed having spots in my life.

Poko Heyokah, which means "little clown god" in Spanish and Lakota Sioux, walked into our house and licked the cats on the head. Our family was whole again. He became a huge beach bum. Running down the empty beaches where I used to live on Long Island, he was in heaven.

Then I got a job at the Savannah College of Art and Design and we moved to Savannah. The boxes came out and the dog got depressed. I kept telling him, "You're coming with us." But I don't think he believed me until we actually got in the car and drove seventeen hours to our new home. It was tough the first few weeks. We kept trying to find dog-friendly beaches and got a ticket on Tybee for our efforts. The dog moped around the house. Then we discovered Forsyth Park, the Savannah Dog Park, and the neighborhood children started a Poko Fan Club. They come over in the afternoons to see if Poko can come out to play. As he scratches his back in the grass and plays with his cats, he knows he's safe. As long as we are all together—we are our home.

HEATHER DUNE MACADAM

CASEY

I said I could never love another dog again. The pain and despair of watching Pepper and Elsie die after sixteen years with me was simply too much to endure again. Who was I kidding? That lasted only a few years.

My "human children," Nick and Molly, reminded me that the house was just too quiet. Not enough bedlam or dog hair. No soggy licks on the face in the morning or bounding dogs to meet them at the door when they got home from school in the afternoons. Nope, it was just too quiet.

My birthday was just around the corner, and it seemed an appropriate time to get mom another dog. That would be me—"Mom." Molly did the research. She knew the smartest thing would be to select a different type of dog as to not bring back sad memories for her mom, who can't even watch Lassie without crying. She learned her lesson when we watched *Turner and Hooch*. I cried for days after seeing that movie.

No, it had to be a different kind of dog. It was decided that we would start with a puppy, as my husband never had a dog. A puppy seemed a good way to endear him to the specialness of being a doggie daddy. There is nothing like puppy breath and the little round ball of fur nestling under your chin as you watch the Georgia–Georgia Tech game on a Sunday afternoon. Molly and my husband combed the pet ads in the classified section for weeks and finally found what they were looking for.

One Saturday morning I was told we would all be going over to South Carolina to take a look at some eight-week-old puppies. I should have realized then that they had already planned that we would have an extra passenger in the car on the return trip. What better way to bring a new puppy into the home than on a weekend? Lots of time to bond, start potty training, and take scores of pictures of everyone holding the new puppy.

We drove over the bridge to South Carolina and then on to Hardeeville. My husband pulled over to a pay phone and informed me that he was calling the breeder who said he would meet us and "bring us in" to the farm. I thought, "Bring us in? Where is this place? Are we on the back of the moon here or what?" A short time later a big red pickup truck with a huge gun rack pulled into the parking lot. The driver stuck his arm out the window and flagged us to follow him. We drove for at least five miles, turning onto one back road after another. By the time we made the fourth turn, I had no idea where we were. He pulled into what appeared to be a farm and down yet another dirt road. His truck came to an abrupt halt in front of what looked like an old chick coop. He jumped out and strode over to a door, opening it in quick order. Suddenly a blur of legs and fur came tumbling out, one after another. Beagles. Big ones, little ones, freckled ones, quiet ones, rambunctious ones, and all headed straight for us. We were surrounded by a sea of black, white, and brown fur, little warm noses, and the softest ears I've ever felt.

It was a tough decision to make. Not for us. In typical fashion, one puppy chose us. He came up to us and threw himself into my arms. Once I looked into his puppy eyes, I was hooked. My husband then said he wanted to get another one. I thought he meant a different one, and I was ready to fight to keep this little one who had chosen me. What he meant was that he wanted a *second* one. I thought to myself, "He has never wanted to have a dog and now he wants two?" I told him, "Let's just start with one and we can always add to the family later." We did. Three more in the next few years.

Casey became the center of our family. Everyone doted on him, and he lavished love and affection on us in every way imaginable. My husband ordered dog beds—with Casey's name embroidered on them—for almost every room of the house. Lands' End was beginning to know my husband by name. When Don would go on buying trips to New York City, he would come home with "doggie bags" (and I don't mean with food in them) from the latest designer shops on Fifth Avenue. Not for me, but gifts for Casey.

We soon realized with us both working that Casey needed a playmate. Hannah joined us in five months, followed by Clancy, who we rescued from a pet shop. Last but not least, was Gracie. She was a stray I found on the side of the road and brought home. Another beagle. I named her Grace after she was almost hit by six cars the day I found her. She was spared by God's grace, hence her name. It was that day my children told me to have my puppy tubes tied.

Life went on joyfully with our houseful of beagles. We truly did live in the Beagle Bungalow. When Casey was a few years old, he seemed to slow down. I thought he was just settling into being the leader of the pack (us included in that group). I took him to the vet for his usual yearly checkup only to find out he had diabetes. We were, needless to say, very upset at this diagnosis. We feared the end was near for him, and we didn't want to lose him. We loved him so much.

God must have a special place in His heart for pets. It's been six years since Casey has been diagnosed with insulin-dependent diabetes. He rose to the challenge of shots twice a day without batting an eyelash. A few years after his diagnosis he became insulin-resistant and his blood sugars soared into the seven hundreds. IDDM for dogs is very similar, if not identical, to human IDDM. He developed Cushing's disease and seemed to be in a downward spiral. I would wake up at night to follow him outside when he would pee, and I would stick the ketostick under his stream to see if he was in ketosis. A bad sign for him. It must have been a funny sight to my neighbors to see this middle-aged woman chase her dog around the yard in the moonlight and jump down to the ground when he would lift his leg. Yes, a funny, but a loving and devoted, sight. Casey continued to worsen as his vet, Dr. Hazlett, did all in her power to bring him out of it. She contacted the UGA, topped Casey off with a liter of IV fluids, and sent us off in the middle of the day for a last-ditch effort to save him. In my heart I knew she thought he wouldn't make it there. He surprised us all. He lasted through the night and wagged his tail when I came to see him the next day. He had turned the comer. The battle was not over yet though. We had a few more days of stabilization, diagnosis, and plan of treatment. The night before we left UGA he snuggled up to me in the hotel room and looked deep into my eyes for a long time. He seemed to be saying, "Mom, I love you. Thank you for loving me enough to bring me here and give me another chance at being with all of you." He fell asleep in my arms, snuggled as tight as he could be into the hollow of my stomach.

Casey came home the next day. As he sat in the front seat of the car in his new doggie seat belt, there was a peace about him I had never felt before. We were about to begin chemotherapy to bring the Cushing's disease into control. It would be a tough few weeks as he had to be watched closely. We all made it through it, and in true fashion it was tougher on us, the doggie parents, than it was on him.

Blood work came, and he was not at therapeutic levels to control the disease. Back on the massive doses of chemo to bring down his levels. He went for weeks and weeks, amazing his vet and the staff of UGA. We finally did random blood work and discovered he was at therapeutic levels! Dr. Hazlett said Casey should be written up in the journals. There were virtually no side effects from the chemo medication.

That has been almost six months now. Casey is almost blind from the cataracts that so often befall diabetic dogs. I have moved to a new home, and he still bounds around the house as if he were a puppy. He plays like a puppy and acts like a puppy. He is still the leader of the pack and makes sure they all come in from outside in a reasonable time. He is my protector and knows my moods enough to flop down beside me on the couch when I've had a rough day.

Casey has done so much for us. Anyone who has known the love of a pet knows the pain of watching that precious being in sickness. Casey has surpassed everyone's expectation of survival and has not only survived, but lives his live to the fullest. He knows no boundaries and continues to be the comforter in my life. He looks at me every morning when he wakes me up for his shot and seems to say, "Mom, I'm ready for another day. Thank you for taking care of me and for loving me as much as as you do." No, Casey, thank you for loving me as much as you do. You have my heart, and when that day comes when we both meet at Rainbow Bridge, our hearts will join in a circle with my other precious dogs, Pepper, Elsie, and P.J. Then the circle of love will be complete. Love,

THE BEAGLE MOMMY

QUEEN ELIZABETH III ("LIZZY")

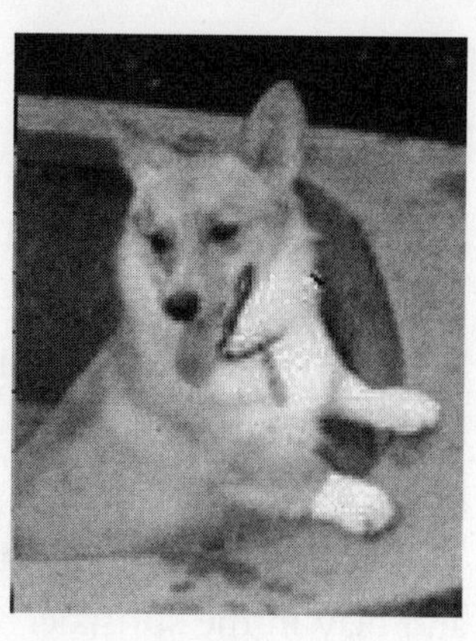

I was born Queen Elizabeth the Third, June 13, eight years ago in Brunswick, Georgia. I am a tricolored Welsh corgi related to those owned by Her Majesty, England's queen.

My mistress tells that at first sight I took forty whacks at her heart, so she calls me Lizzy Borden.

I left my brothers and sisters to live with her in Savannah. She's very special, you know.

Originally I stayed in a big wire house when she was away, watching sunlight on the walls, listening to music, and playing with my sock doll. As soon as she came home we'd chase all through the rooms until I'd land on my furry tutu, finally sliding to a stop at the end of the hall. Then we would do it again.

Mornings were sad times. I lay with my chin on the floor, legs flat out to my sides (like four oars in the water, Grandma said), watching my mistress get ready for work. Our mornings are still the same, except my legs rest against my sides. A girl adds a pound or two growing up.

As I grew I wasn't always a goody girl. I jumped on strangers, chewed new shoes, and napped on a mountain of bed pillows until I heard her car turn onto our street. I ran quickly to get to the door. Each time she leaves she tells me, "Be a good girl. I'll be home in a little while." It is true—she always comes back. As quick as the door shuts, she stoops and we hug a lot.

I don't get on the bed now. Instead I chase squirrels and play in the sprinkler. Auto travel is my thing, too. Long after I've been to a place, I remember it and know where I am.

I don't like *cats*, nor others like me. Not even Nancy Lucy, who lives next door. We are much alike—she doesn't know she is a dog either.

I do have lots of people friends—children and those who come and go making sure that I'm safe inside the gate or don't get stepped on.

The postman, I tolerate. He parks a block away, but I can judge just how long it will take him to drop mail into our slot, then it is okay for me to bark. Are you curious about my character? I'm independent, proud, very smart, protective, and a dainty eater. I am loving to those I choose to love. Unique. Unlike any other. Just

Lizzy

Clancy Melroy ("Clancy")

When our son Chris's mother in law, Betty Reed, called that evening and said that she had the cutest little Shih Tzu puppy that needed a new home, I knew what the answer would be. We had just lost our sixteen-year-old cocker pooh, Mandy, who was our loyal pro-tector and shadow to our eight-year-old bassett hound, Shamus.

There had to be a reason, however, why Betty insisted on making the thirty-mile trip to our house that evening rather than us picking it up the next day. She did not mention that we would be the third owner. Of course the blond puppy was adorable and immediately ran to my wife, Judy, and jumped, wagged, and licked. Her next trick was to urinate on the rug. "She must be excited," mused Betty, with the same look as an Edsel salesman after making a sale.

The next day we got all the needed items for "Clancy," also the name of a blond cocker pooh we had for many years. That night, after returning home from a wake service and standing in the rain while Clancy "did his thing," Clancy ran to the driveway of the house next door looking for the two Shih Tzus that lived there. As I grumbled to myself when Clancy did not come back, when I reached down to pick him up he darted down the driveway, made a quick left turn toward home, and ran right down the storm sewer. After hearing the splash, I ran into our house and grabbed a flashlight while frantically telling Judy what was happening. I reached the sewer and was able to remove the top to see Clancy swimming in circles. If he headed down one of the pipes, I knew he would be gone, so I took off my trousers and shoes and jumped in. Just as I grabbed him, Judy arrived, whisked him into the house, and had him bathed and blow-dried by just about the time I got out of the shower.

Seeing Judy cuddling Clancy in that warm towel with both still shaking, I know Clancy winked at me to indicate that no matter how many chewed baseboards and holes in the wall and sprinkling on rugs that were to follow, he would never be evicted from Judy's home.

Donald and Judy Melroy

174

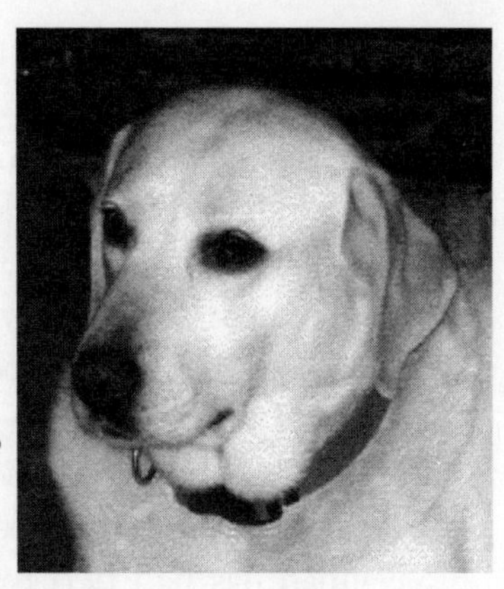

ADPG Shine on Savannah, CD, CGC, UCD ("Savannah")

We bought Savannah, sight unseen, on the telephone because I was so impressed with her pedigree. She was from the oldest Lab kennel in the United States, Shamrock Acres in Illinois. We picked her up on Valentine's Day 1993. My first impression when I saw her was complete disappointment. I thought that she was the ugliest Lab pup I had ever seen. I was committed, so I hid my feelings, glued on a smile, wrapped up my ugly duckling, and left for home. I waited seven months to register her because I had my doubts as to her true heritage. The only things that she had going for her were that she came house-trained, never jumped, didn't chew anything but her toys, and came when she was called. (A few more reasons for my doubts.)

I had time to do more research on her line, since I wasn't in a hurry to show her, and I found out that Labs mature very slowly. Savannah definitely was a late bloomer. She was finally ready for her debut at two and a half years of age. She had turned into the most beautiful Labrador retriever I have ever had. She mothered three beautiful litters and was the perfect mom.

Savannah has helped work with children, adults, and other canines that have dog issues. Savannah helps new handlers in our training classes at Carol's Pampered Pets. I have always said to my students, "I can teach your dogs patience, but I can't teach you patience." There is always that one exception. Savannah—and my mom, Blanche—have taught me patience and not to judge a book by its cover.

Savannah has had two major cancer surgeries and has come back each time with renewed love of life. I guess she still has some mothering and nurturing to do. She is a great nursemaid for her daughter Anna, who has made it through two TPLO surgeries (knee replacements), and she was my hospice angel for Polly, her best friend that we lost February 14, 2004, and Max, lost May 12, 2004.

Thank you, Savannah, for all that you have taught us. Special thanks to her vets, Dr. Billy Sanders and Dr. Pam Fandrich. We love you.

CAROL AND JON
AND SIBLINGS
ANNA, SUMMER, SARGEANT, AND HUNTER

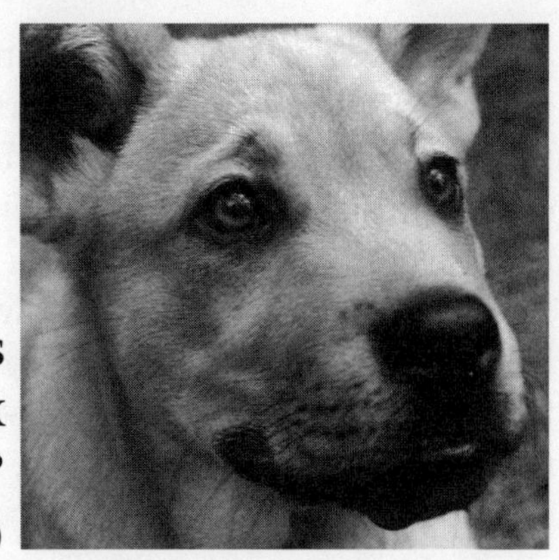

DUDERONIMUS TRUAX ("DUDE," "SCHPUDA")

I was rescued in 2001 by Luke Truax and Jessica Pope, my loving parents. Thanks to them, I live a very exciting dog life. I am a Carolina dog–Chow-Chow mix, and people often comment on how beautifully unique I look. It must be my cool spotted tongue and cute underbite.

During my short life I have traveled extensively, to my parents' original homes and beyond. I enjoy a change of scenery, but love Savannah because of the great parks, sandy soil, and ever-present mud puddles. Fort Pulaski also is a favorite spot for me—so many smells and long walks. I have good friends in Savannah, such as my favorite pal, Hamish Goff-Rixon [see pages 125–26], whom I've known since I was a pup. I've also enjoyed the time I've spent in Connecticut and Idaho, where my parents came from. I love to hike and explore the vast terrain of those places, where I also have made friends, including Sunflower, Althea, and Jupiter, who are my partners-in-crime when I visit. We pass the time by lying in the sun, going to the beach, and playing keep-away with our precious bones.

I am very obedient, which makes it easy for my parents to take me practically everywhere. Car rides are the best, especially fast ones, where I can stick my face out of the window and feel the wind flip-flop my jowls and dry out my eyes. I love that.

I know that I am a very lucky, special dog who is loved tremendously. I hope that my life is continuously full of car-chasing, lake-swimming, and human kisses.

With a paw shake and a wet dog kiss, I am,

DUDE

MS. BOGEY'S
SKIDAWAY

When you grow up the daughter of a veterinarian, animals are a given. Many dogs and cats have come and gone, but all are remembered fondly. After each loss the "I never want to go through that heartbreak again" reverberates over and over. It will never cease to amaze me how quiet a house can be when there are no animals.

When we moved from Atlanta to Savannah, we thought about another dog, but never got around to the search. Last August I received a call from our oldest son (on behalf of the other two sons), asking what I thought about getting Dad a dog for Christmas. Without hesitation I said yes. Now, what breed? The families have an assortment—shelty, Lhasa apso, and a golden retriever. Since they had the idea and they were making the purchase, they got to choose.

We went to Atlanta for Thanksgiving and for an early Christmas present, unbeknownst to Dad. They made the decision not to present her until we were ready to leave on Sunday. Needless to say, I had to contain my excitement and keep the secret for another three days. The boys and their families really made this a production. They made a video of the day they all got in their cars, complete with five grandchildren, and drove to the breeders to pick out the special surprise.

The families got Dad into the den under the pretense of watching a video. I was a little unsure of what Dad's reaction would be. It ended up being worth the price of admission. It's not too often you can make a grown man cry (or a least misty-eyed). He was delighted, to say the least. Now came the big argument of who was going to drive and who was going to get the pleasure of the new bundle of joy with puppy breath! We split the drive.

Ms. Bogey's Skidaway, a golden retriever, is the love of our lives. Didn't know there could be so many Kodak moments—just like your first child. We almost forgot how much work is involved in raising another puppy. But we wouldn't trade one dog hair, one oops on the carpet, all the midnight walks, vet visits, dog washes, or obedience classes not to have her in our lives. Hopefully for many, many, many years.

TRISH POTTS

Richard Russell Wilmington McAbee ("Rusty")

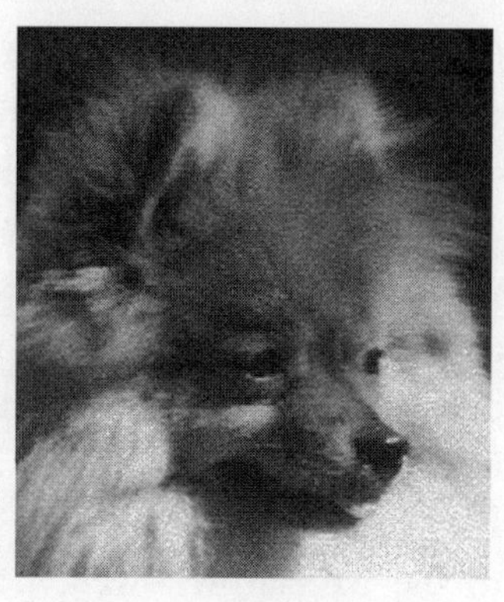

Rusty is a handsome, feisty, one-year-old purebred Pomeranian who enjoys keeping his mom busy chasing after him! I met Rusty when he was five weeks old, and I fell in love with him immediately. Rusty's great-grandparents, Lamar and Amy Salter, took me to Jesup to Cherub Acres in September 2003. Cherub Acres is owned by Sylvia Smith, a breeder who loves and cherishes her Pomeranians. I was very pleased with her facility, and was very pleased with Rusty when I picked him up. He was so small—only three pounds, he fit in the palm of my hand, and he had such baby-fine fur, it was like holding a fluffy ball of cashmere. He immediately stole our hearts when he puttered over to us, looked at us with his little eyes, and nudged our feet because he was too little to do anything else. He still employs this technique (although there are a lot of kisses involved as well) to get out of any trouble he finds himself in.

When I took Rusty home that first night, his grandmother, Janeen McAbee, was more pleased than I had ever hoped she would be. You see, the whole rea-son I wanted a dog was because I was going to be entering Mercer Medical School in the fall of 2004. In fall 2003 I told my parents that I wanted to have a dog so that I would have someone with me at medical school. I had researched dogs for a few weeks, but I hadn't really set my heart on anything. So, when I went to see Rusty, my parents weren't sure that I was actually serious. However, when I walked through that door with Rusty, my mother melted and fell in love as fast as my grandmother and I had. Rusty's Uncle Ricky fell in love as well, and has been so much help to us! My father—well, he's not in love, but I think he's happier now that he doesn't have to deal with a dog he never wanted in the first place.

After that first night, I learned what having a dog meant—the multiple attempts to train him for the litterbox, the unyielding barking, the chewing, the biting, and the unconditional love that you can receive from the most precious pet in the world.

Since September 2003 Rusty and I have been a team. Every day he does something that makes me smile, whether it is falling over a pillow, jumping up in my lap to give me kisses, or running all over the apart-ment looking for a toy when he hears someone squeak a dog toy on TV. Rusty is my joy, my friend, and my companion at medical school. Whenever I have a bad day, I know that he will be home waiting for me. He jumps up and down, so eager for me to pick him up, so eager for me to just be at home with him while he tackles his stuffed panda bear that is bigger than he is, so eager to fall asleep on the couch next to me. He is, and will always be, my best friend.

JESSICA MCABEE

182

I am a Keeshond and I am twelve years old. I live in a tall building in New York City with many other dogs and humans, including my humans, Nina and Fred. Nina is a violinist, and Fred orders food. Fred and Nina have humans of their own, and Fred's humans live with a Savannah dog named Sarah.

I want to express my thanks to Minnie Beil for the privilege of appearing in this book. She graciously decided that since I am in love with Sarah I can have a place here. You may have already read about Sarah [see *Savannah Dogs*, pages 344-46]. She was rescued. I can't explain it, but when Sarah comes to visit, I just can't keep my paws off her! She is the only dog I want to play with, even though my building is full of other dogs. I am always feeling compelled to show her how much I like her—I think I love her! Maybe it's because she's a Savannah dog.

When Sarah's not visiting, Nina gives me lots of snacks and Fred walks me and brushes my coat out, and I get to bark at the doorbell, and the neighbor's doorbell, and the elevator, and the clothes washer, and the telephone. Sometimes I can knock the receiver off

the cradle and I get to bark at the telemarketer, or
Fred's boss, or whomever else might be calling! I also
have to supervise their meals to make sure everything
gets eaten. The rest of the time, I sleep, which is very
tiring.

CHARLIE

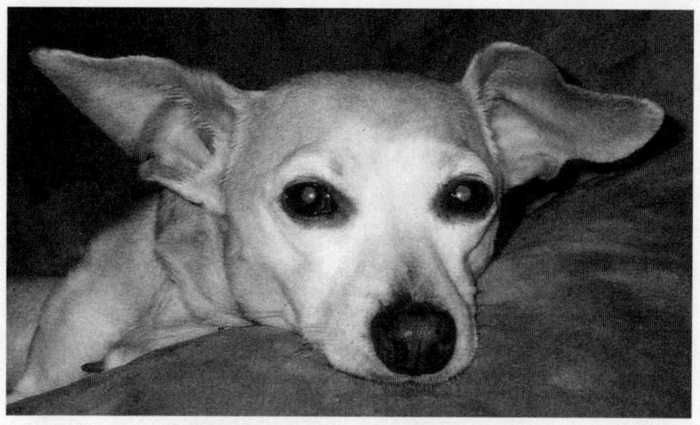

ROXY MCSILBERMANN
("ROXY," "ROX")

"It was a dark and stormy night. "That's how Snoopy, that bold beagle, started his novel. But in my case—no offense, Snoopy—it's true. It was a dark and stormy night.

It was December 31, 2002, and it was raining cats and . . . You'll excuse me if I leave out the last part of that idiom. I don't like to think of my fellow four-legged friends falling from the sky. Anyway, it was raining cats and was very, very cold. I had been wandering around for a long time, with only the chain around my neck, when I spotted a house with lots of lights on. A neighborhood cat named Smoky took one look at me, saw my ribs showing and my body shaking, and told me that I might find shelter there.

Sure, I was scared. But I was too cold, wet, tired, and hungry not to give it a try. I knew I had to make a bold move. I went up to a door that had lots of window panes in it, stood up on my hind legs, and looked in the window. I thought the people inside saw me, but I wasn't sure. So I ran around to the side of the house, climbed up on an old piece of furniture, and peeked in another window. This time I knew they saw me.

I tried to look sad and it wasn't too hard; I was sad and lonely. They didn't let me in, but they put a warm blanket on that old piece of furniture and I stayed there for the night. I figured it was better than some of the other places I'd been sleeping, and it sheltered me from the rain.

The next day the people took me in. They fed me, gave me a bath, and made me get these shots I didn't like. I was worried at first because I didn't know these people. But it wasn't long before I had names for them: Mommy and Daddy.

They told me I could stay under three conditions: *no* getting on the furniture; *no* getting on the bed; and *no* people food. It didn't take long, though. Now I own every piece of furniture in the house, I snuggle under the covers with my parents every night, and get a few scraps after supper. They spoil me rotten and I love every minute of it.

My parents still don't know where I came from, and to tell you the truth, I don't think about it anymore. I have a real home now, and people that love and take good care of me.

Yep, it was a dark and stormy night—and New Year's Eve, no less. But there was lots of sunshine just beyond those clouds, and the promise of a new life—my new life.

ROXY

186

Belle Slemons

I'm a beagle mix, but what else is in the mix is any-body's guess! My mom and dad suspect that part of the mix may be cat, since I love to lounge in the sun, sit on the back of the couch staring out the window, and lick my paws clean. And, oh yeah, I really enjoy playing with cats. My brother, who is full cat, doesn't feel the same way about me, but true to my nature, I love him anyway.

My dad rescued me from a shelter in Atlanta just in the nick of time, and I've made his life happier every day he's had me.

I love my toys, especially my Kong and tennis-ball-on-a-rope. When my dad comes home from work and plays with me, I can't get enough and tug the rope with all my might.

If I hear a cheese wrapper, better get out of my way because I'll come running. I eat all kinds of things that I'm not supposed to, including carrots, apples, and my brother the cat's food.

For a long time I was a landlocked dog, but here in Savannah I get to do all kinds of fun things, including my first swim. I'm a little waterlogged in my picture, but that's because I'd just gotten out of the marsh for the first time. I like all kinds of water, except when I'm getting a bath.

My parents say the best thing about me is my sweet nature. I love everyone (and every food) I've ever met. I let you know how much I love you by giving lots of kisses and smiling at you. They also say I'm smart, maybe too smart. When Mom puts on her tennis shoes, I know we're going for a walk and run toward the door. When Dad gets out the leash, I tap dance with excitement.

More than anything, I love to sniff. Every day holds some new scent on which I want to get my nose. After a rain I run outside to smell the changes brought on by the falling leaves and rain. During a walk I stop a thousand times to see what might be new. My nose serves me well, and my mom thinks it cute when I wiggle it as I sniff.

I'm just full of love, trust, and enjoyment, and I can't wait to get to play with all my dog and cat friends and cousins.

BELLE

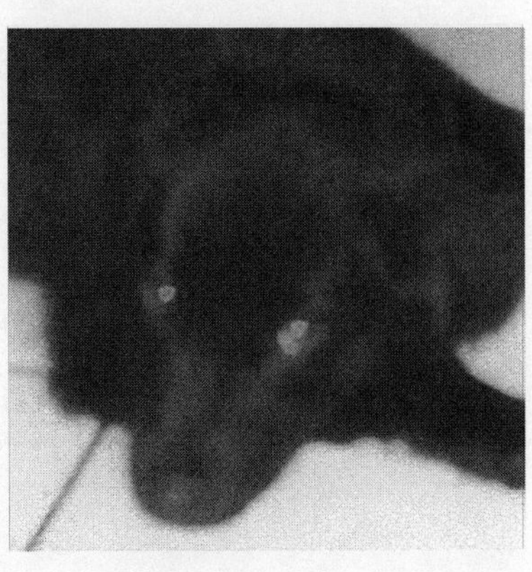

SASHA

She may not be Gennifer Flowers, but the young lady is quite striking. We met last month on the beach at sunset. I was alone, and as she approached I could not help but notice her long-legged, slim body and doleful eyes. I did not expect to have an actual encounter, but as the young lady made a decided path toward my beach chair, I quickly realized that an exchange would shortly ensue. To my surprise, not a word was uttered. We merely exchanged glances. I offered an open quizzical smile as her dolorous, piercing eyes fixed on mine. We were both momentarily transfixed. Could I possibly become involved in an awkward summer romance?

I could! She is the epitome of femininity, charm, and warmth, and without a moment's hesitation became "the other woman" in my life. Sasha, a ten-week-old black Australian border collie is now part of the gayest ménage à trois ever conceived by any radical, philandering, graying gentleman with a romantic heart!

MICHAEL SOTTILE

189

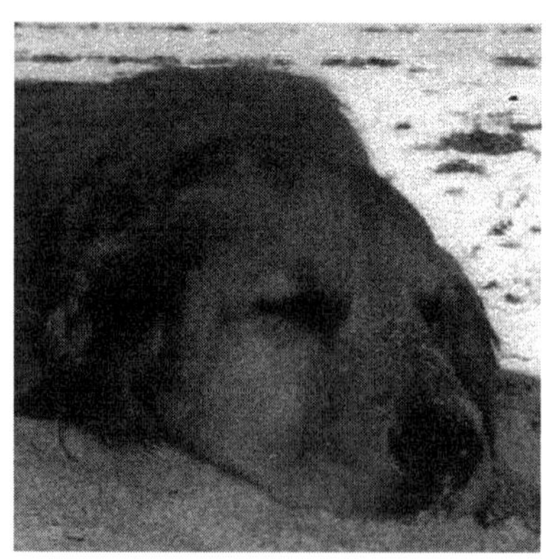

PHOENIX

He was a two-time loser. Picked up in metro Atlanta running free, he had been given a second chance, this time in Athens with a veterinarian's assistant. After he got into some antifreeze, she decided that he was too much trouble. He was back inside. New Year's weekend 2001. With the holiday weekend and the high number of dogs in the pound, he had only twenty-four hours before he would be "euthanatized."

I was at work on January 2, much earlier than usual, although I'm not sure why. I got a phone call from a colleague saying his car had broken down and he needed a ride back to his house. Why he didn't need to get to work, I still don't know. He lived on the other side of town from me (near the animal shelter), so I didn't get over that way very often. As I was returning to work, I suddenly decided to go by the shelter.

Although my wife, daughter, and I had been talking about getting another dog as company for our slightly neurotic, exceedingly sweet, rescued Lab mix, we weren't really looking that hard. We knew that it would be difficult to find a dog with just the right temperament to complement our loving, formerly abused Grace.

190

As I walked around the cages, I saw a very dirty, very thin golden retriever. With his large head and sad but sweet eyes, he was beautiful. I asked to see him. He was so happy to be out of his cage, but he wouldn't look at me and he didn't wag his tail. He just leaned against me, getting me filthy. Yet I knew that this was the dog for us. When I called my wife, Tammy, I said, "I found your dog." Like me, she fell in love with him on sight.

Over the next several months, Phoenix gained weight and strength. After a couple of months, he started wagging a little. Then we noticed that he would look at our faces when we spoke to him. Always, he wanted attention. He wanted to be in the room with us. He wanted love. He would even jump like a kangaroo when we got home in the evening!

Still, whenever we left the house, Phoenix chewed something—newspapers, wicker baskets, rugs. He even ate a page from my Bible. Hungry for the Word, I guess! In June we took a trip to the beach, as usual bringing our dogs with us. On our second day at the beach, Phoenix, presumably, tore the screen out of the screened porch. My fault, I said. We forgot to leave the door propped open. A couple of days later, Phoenix took off running down the beach, running in his goofy, loping run as fast as he could. We caught up to him when he stopped to see some kids, his favorite kind of people.

This was hardly his first time running. He never seemed to be running from us, he seemed to be looking for something. He always seemed surprised and glad to see us when we caught up to him. Later that week as we walked down the beach one evening, I told my wife, "That's it. I can't handle him anymore." She was distraught, having fallen head over heels for Phoenix.

But after returning home, it crossed my mind to search the web about dog behavior. I found a lot of information on a condition called "separation anxiety." The articles described our dog exactly. We asked our vet about a medicine called Clomipramine. He gave us some to try and, voilà! no more chewing. No more running and looking. He wasn't lethargic, didn't appear "drugged."

That was over three years ago. Today Phoenix is ninety-five pounds, happy, and healthy. We learned that around fifty percent of the dogs in the pound have separation anxiety. It is so hard to deal with because the dogs are great when you are home and are destructive only when you are gone. When we realized that Phoenix was nervous, anxious, and scared when we were gone, we felt so badly for him. Medication is only one of the ways to treat this condition. If you have some extra love, some patience and understanding, think about saving a sweet, loving dog like our Phoenix. They will be forever grateful and fill your life with unconditional loyalty.

JIM SULLIVAN

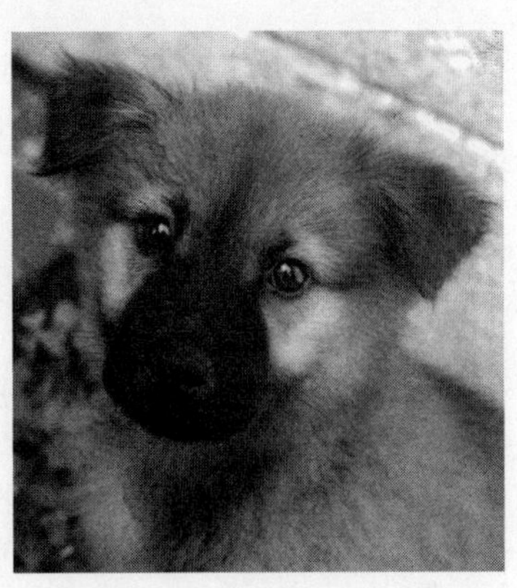

ROSCOE

The alarm buzzed bright and early one summer morning. The clock read seven o'clock and I had to be at work at seven thirty. Feeling rushed, I jumped out of bed and quickly prepared myself for the day I had before me. As I stepped out my front door my jaw dropped at the sight of a black-and-tan puppy. Time stopped when I saw her, and I looked around to see if she had come from a neighboring house. It was hard to believe she had come out of nowhere. She looked overly zealous to see me, and without hesitation began to lick and playfully nibble on my hand. Her coat was extremely soft and fluffy, although her belly was swollen and her neck was bare without a collar or any tags. After our greetings I went inside to retrieve some water, but no food. As I laid down the water, I realized I was running late to work, so without any binding for the dog I left her on the front porch and hoped to see her when I returned home.

My shift at work seemed long, but it was only three and a half hours. After work I rushed home to see if my visitor was still there. Before I reached the driveway, I slowly pulled up as if not to startle the puppy. To my surprise and great delight, she was lying down

193

under my porch between the widths of my front door. She did not get up eagerly to greet me. Instead she slowly stretched, rolled over, and licked me her hellos.

Her water bowl was empty, and she appeared very hungry, so we took a drive to PetSmart. In the car she snuggled next to my leg and enjoyed the full blast of the air conditioner after lying in that Savannah heat. I bought her some food and set up a doctor's appointment for her, but was still not sure if I would keep her. I held her the whole time we were in the store, her head underneath my chin, her paws wrapped around my neck. I certainly did feel a connection with her, and after much deliberation between the pros and cons of having such a huge responsibility, I decided to keep her. Ever since that day, time for me has never been the same, and it stops every time I see her face.

EMILIE TUMINELLA

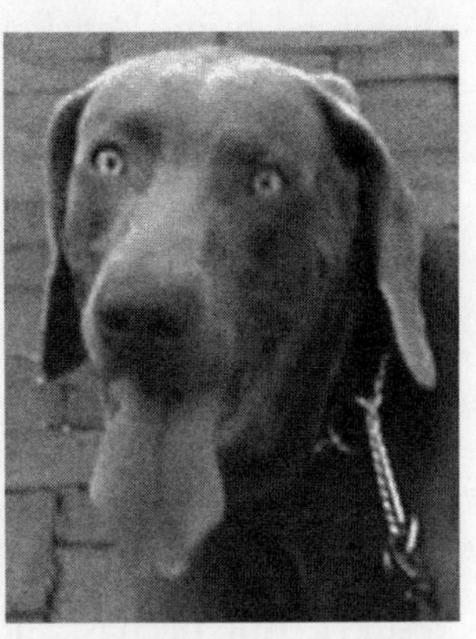

Jackson Archer Vanlerberghe ("Jackson")

Though Jackson has been an integral part of my family since October 2003, he has done a lot of moving around and affecting the lives of those with whom I have lived as well. During the eleven months he has lived with me, we have also shared our different residences with seven other loving roommates (not simultaneously), who were certainly at least as attached to Jackson as they were to me. When our former roommates Sarah and Joel made their way across Ardsley Park for a surprise visit in August to announce that Joel had finally popped the question and to celebrate their recent engagement, everyone, including the pup, was thrilled.

As my roommates old and new sat around discussing the wedding and all the necessary arrangements, Jackson could be heard wrestling with something, busy in the other room, but I had just moved into a new home and couldn't think of anything valuable that he would be getting into that needed to be saved from him. Since we were all rather captivated by the wedding details, we let him be; we didn't hear any crashes or catastrophes. The future bride and groom discussed how they had two flower girls in mind, but no ring bearer. Since I was to be a bridesmaid, it naturally occurred to me that Jackson should be the obvious frontrunner in the category of handsome attendants, as he had been a prominent, important young male in both of their lives.

Jackson, however, is a little wild. He is sweet and admittedly a bit of a mama's boy, and I can't imagine he would ever intentionally hurt a person unless I were in danger (this actually fortunately has not been tested). But he has a lot of energy, like others of his weimaraner breed, and despite his sweet demeanor and need to snuggle, he has a fierce bark that would certainly intimidate a church full of wedding guests, particularly if he were nervous or I was already down the aisle and could not walk him.

In any event, as if on cue, when the topic comically arose about Jackson filling this position for their ceremony and about all the mishaps that might ensue if he were to take on this responsibility, my shiny, silver, blue-eyed puppy gallantly trotted into the living room and weaved his way past each of the room's inhabitants carrying a wiry yellow object in his mouth. It was an Easter basket that my parents had sent him in April, but that he hadn't given much more than a moment's notice to since taking all of the toys out of it four months earlier. He was carrying it by the handle in his mouth, and I really think he was smiling, a true audition for a captive audience. As he paraded among the current and former roommates looking proudly from face to face, we all laughed and decided we had never seen a more apparent plea to be included in a critical position on Sarah and Joel's special day, and we considered his not-so-subtle action as his official offer of his services.

Fortunately Sarah and Joel know Jackson well enough not to trust him to behave calmly in a crowd at a somewhat solemn occasion. Though he is often touted a "handsome devil," he always lives up to the attractiveness part, but just as frequently fits the bill for the latter half of that title as well. There will be no ring bearer.

Julia Vanlerberghe

197

I am an energetic, spunky, and good-looking two-year-old Boston terrier. Although Bostons are generally better suited for cooler climates, I am a true Southern boy at heart. I love down-home cooking, and I am a natural at exhibiting Southern hospitality. I enjoy long walks on the beach and quiet evenings at home. My favorite pastimes include hunting for crabs, walking in Forsyth Park, chasing hopping frogs, and traveling anywhere in the car.

My days are filled with lots of free time to do what I want. I usually begin my mornings with a brisk walk and a light breakfast. Mom and Dad both work during the day, so I rule the house. What am I talking about—I always rule the house. I have a pretty nice set-up at home. I have my own comfy chair to lounge and sleep on and a large window to survey the yard for squirrels and birdies. Most days I sleep on my chair or chew on my toys until Mom gets home. Then we take another walk and visit some of my doggy friends in the neighborhood.

Some days I accompany Dad to work. I try not to be a distraction for him, but most people just can't resist my good looks and appealing demeanor. If I demonstrate professional doggy behavior, Dad will take me for a burger at lunch. I tend to become a disruption after lunch with my snoring and snorting during nap time. It forces Dad and his coworkers to put on headphones to escape the noise. Nonetheless everyone is sad to see me go at quitting time.

My favorite days are spent at my own personal day spa. I get the works. A full body rubdown complete with a vichy shower by Mom, warm-towel dry compliments of Dad, my nails clipped, my ears cleaned, and my teeth brushed. Afterward I feel great, and I make sure to parade and prance around the house so Mom and Dad can see my new do.

At night we play with one of my many toys housed in my toy bin. If Mom or Dad doesn't feel like playing with the toy I have brought them, I keep bringing other toys until they get interested. If they still don't feel like playing with me, then I steal anything I can get my teeth on. I'm not picky; socks, dryer sheets, even underwear will do. That always seems to get them excited.

My favorite time of the day has got to be bedtime because if I don't get my beauty rest I can get very grumpy. I consider myself to be a very generous puppy because I allow Mom and Dad to share the bed with me. Normally I wait for Mom to get ready and then I attack her with kisses, on the lips of course. I prefer to sleep under the covers right next to Dad. I like to share his pillow.

I am very excited to be in this edition of *Savannah Dogs*. It is my first small step toward gracing the cover of *GQ* someday.

Murphy

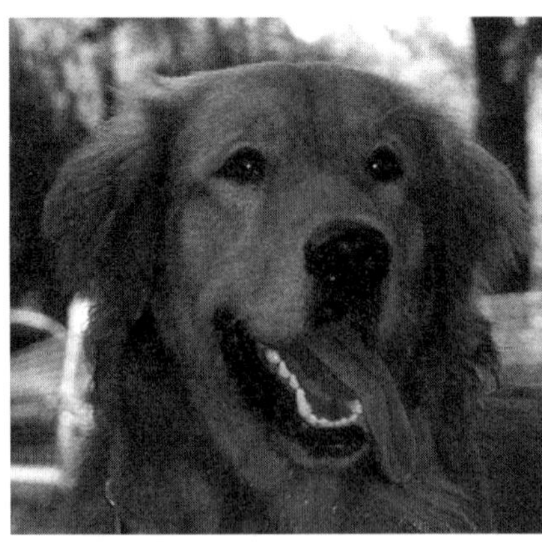

MARSHALL
XIII
("MARSHALL")

Hi! Do you want to play Frisbee? I learned how to play Frisbee right here in Forsyth Park almost four years ago. I started by fetching a ball, and over time I learned how to jump high in the air to catch my Frisbee. I was born here in Savannah, and at that time we lived on Jones Street. I loved walking to Forsyth Park every day. Sometimes my dad would take me to work, and I got to play with the Rangers. They loved to watch me catch my ball, but most of all they loved to play tug. I would run and hike with them in the morning, and I even learned how to swim with them out on Hunter.

I love swimming. Fetching my retriever in the water makes people really happy, too. No matter how far they throw it, I'll get it for them. Sometimes my dad takes me to the beach. I love playing in the sand. It's so soft to run in, and everyone cheers when I jump to catch my Frisbee. When I get hot I just jump in the water and catch some of the waves to cool down or I'll dig a hole under my dad to get out of the sun. My dad and I run or hike every morning. I am really fast. When I was three my dad took me to a 5k race for

200

dogs in Wilmington, North Carolina, and we won. It was close, but right at the end, when my dad said, "Okay, Marshall, let's win this thing," I just kicked it in and we sailed past the competition. I'm a fast dog. I love running with my dad.

One day my dad had to go really far away for work, and I couldn't go with him. He was gone for a long time, and I had to stay with his mom and dad. I didn't want him to go, but he said he had to because it was really important work and he promised to come back for me. I missed him so much. I loved living with my grandparents though. They fed me lots of good food, and they took me for walks every day. I missed my dad and Savannah a lot and wish I could have gone to work with him.

Then one evening, while I was sleeping on the porch, I woke up and there he was. He was a lot skinnier, but that was him. I jumped up on him and gave him a big hug, then I grabbed my Frisbee and I showed him I could still do all my tricks. I rolled, sat and lay down, stood up, played dead, and shook. I also gave him a high-five. I was so happy; I was with my daddy again! And there was someone else too—a girl. He told me that we were all going back to Savannah together. I was going to miss my grandparents because they were so good to me, but I was ready to go back home to Savannah.

We got there and went right back to Forsyth Park. There were so many familiar smells. And I met some new dog friends to play with, and I even made friends with a bunch of kids who love the park as much as I do. They don't throw my Frisbee as far as the big people do, but I love hearing them laugh and cheer when I catch it for them. My dad and I moved into a new house on Gaston Street, and it's so close to the park, I can smell it from my window. Every day my dad and his girlfriend take me out to play Frisbee. I love spending time with my dad's new girlfriend. She loves to play with me and take me swimming. She has two kitties that love to play hide-and-seek too. She's so nice to me. We all have so much fun together, going for walks downtown and playing in the park. I love Savannah so much. Savannah is where I was born, and Savannah is where I met my new mommy.

MARSHALL

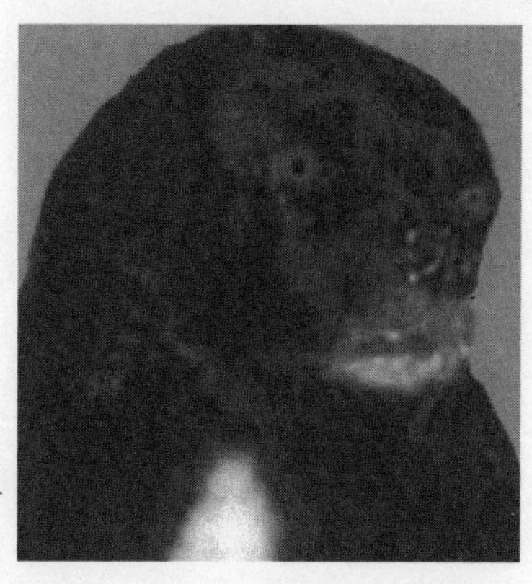

Missy may not be a thoroughbred, but that doesn't really matter to us. She's our dog, and we love her *almost* as much as she loves us. We got her one day when a young mother came up to our car as we were driving through a trailer park. In desperation, the woman asked, "Can you please take my dog? My husband re-cently left me and I have no way to take care of my puppy." To be honest, we hesitated for a moment, but our five-year-old son, Mark, had recently arrived from the Philippines and he really needed a friend. Missy was just what the doctor ordered, so we took her home and have never regretted the decision to make her a part of our family.

Missy is not just a loving dog, she is also very intelligent. Not long after we took her home, she learned to paw at the back door to let us know she needed to do her business. Once her business is done, she comes back to the door, standing sideways as she wags her tail to knock on the door. When she comes back in the house, she goes straight to the can of treats in our pantry and points with her nose at the can. If that doesn't get our attention, she turns her head to look at us, wags her tail, and paws at the floor until we look at her. Next she points again at the can asking for a treat. Once she gets it, she dashes to the living room and eats it slowly. Sometimes she even moans during the enjoyment of having her special treat. When she's thirsty, she goes to her cup in the master bedroom. If the cup is empty, she'll do similar things, as she does with the treats, in order to let us know she is thirsty.

Missy loves everybody in the house, but she really loves Papa Derell the most because she follows him everywhere. In fact she's lying next to Papa Derell even now as he types this story on the computer. Sometimes she likes to get in the bed with Mama Eden and Papa Derell, but there's really not enough room in the bed for the three of us to sleep comfortably. Recently she's been sleeping in Mark's bed, but she'd really rather be in the bedroom with Mama and Papa.

Missy loves to play ball with anyone in the family who is willing. When she picks up her ball, she wants someone to take it away from her, but they have to fight to get it from her. Once someone gets the ball from her, she tries to get it back. When we throw the ball across the room or down the hall, she races to get it and then brings it back. But, again, she wants us to chase her and fight to take it away.

Missy is a real treasure to have around. Needless to say, she's *very special* to us.

DERRELL WALDHAUER

Zorro

H! This is my literary debut. Mom doesn't know it, but I have been watching her use this computer to do her schoolwork for hours on end, and I have *finally* figured out how to use it. So, when Mr. Beil asked me to write my story, I pounced on the idea because it fits in perfectly with my master plan to write a Pulitzer prize–winning story and make so much money that I could spoil my mom for a change. Here goes. I hope you like it.

I am a three-year-old Borzoi. A lot of people don't recognize the breed because there are not many of us around Savannah, but when Mom tells them that I have also been called a Russian wolfhound, they seem to understand. I am black and white with long, somewhat curly fur, stand about thirty-two inches tall at the shoulder (according to Mom), and am built to run like the wind. Oh, and people always say that I look regal. I may look regal, but that doesn't stop me from playing with all the other dogs at my day-care center.

I also *love* to play with my plush toys, especially the ones that sound like animals. I used to have a lamb, but it stopped making noise, so Mom got me a cow that moos. Oh, and I also *love* to chew on rawhide and Milk-Bones. My favorite place is in Mom's bed. I'm not supposed to have bones in her bed, but it is just so comfy. Besides, what does she think that I am going to do with the Milk-Bones that she scatters around the house before she leaves? I lie in her bed all day eating bones and watching "Animal Planet." I have a good life.

Mom has started trying to teach me lure coursing. It's fun to chase the "rabbit." (It's really just a plastic bag, they are *not* fooling me, but I'll go along with them and call it a "rabbit.") The only problem with this lure coursing is that I am afraid I may get in trouble for chasing this rabbit, like I do when I chase the three cats at home. Mom says it's okay, but I think it may be a trick. We'll have to wait and see how that goes.

Wow! Time sure does fly when you're writing. It's almost time for Mom to come home, and I haven't even been able to tell you about how I rescued those puppies from a brush fire and saved that kitten from drowning. Oh, well, guess I'll save those stories for the sequel, or for Lassie.

Thanks for reading my story, and be sure to say "Hi" if you see me walking around town with my mom. I may be a little shy when I first meet you, but Mom says that I'm a ham once I get to know some-one. I'm not sure what that means, but I would like a piece of ham if you have one.

Z

GRATEFUL JAKE

He sure didn't look like a lucky dog on that February afternoon—filthy, skinny, and scared, he was dragging fifteen feet of chain hooked around his neck and running down the middle of Bull Street during the evening rush hour. But this was his lucky day. Linda Howard spotted him and told her daughter to pull her car over to the curb, and in a minute that grubby dog was in the backseat of the nice clean Audi.

And if this wasn't lucky enough, consider who picked him up: Linda and Don Howard run the White Bluff Veterinary Hospital, and that evening he had a clean cage, a badly needed bath, and dinner. They called him "Scout," and Doctor Don diagnosed a bad case of heartworm and started treatment right away. Advertisements in the local paper didn't bring a call from his owners, and Scout started to settle in, but three months later he was still there. Everybody liked Scout, but somebody needed to give this dog a home—the veterinary already has more than its share of mascots.

We'd just bought a small house and decided we could get a dog. We met Doctor Don the same week, and he said we should come down to White Bluff that

Saturday to meet Scout, and we took him for a test drive in Forsyth Park. He was eager to please, biddable, and ready to say hello to everyone—and every dog—in the park. We decided that the name "Jake" would suit him better than "Scout," but there was one more all-important stop to make that day: our house, which we share with three cats.

Fang hid under the bed, but we have two huge Maine coon cats, Booger T. and Bubba. At twenty pounds, Bubba is formidable, and his brother Booger arched and puffed up and hissed and looked as ferocious as possible. Booger's low growl was not likely to be mistaken for a feline "G'day, mate." Jake lay down and rolled over. "I don't want to take over, fellas, I just want a home." He'd passed the cat test, and he became "Grateful Jake" soon after we brought him home. He was clearly happy to have a family, and Jake learned to treat each cat differently. He lets Fang box his nose while Jake pretends to nip him. He lies around amiably with lazy old Bubba, and treats Booger just as you'd treat any other space alien. Later we got Grateful Jake a black-and-white "tuxedo" kitten from the Richmond Hill animal shelter. He's unmistakably Jake's kitten, and we named him Elwood.

Jake rightly regards downtown Savannah as his home, and goes out of his way to greet citizens and tourists alike when we walk him around River Street. He especially watches for tourists who are lonely for their dogs at home. He's happy to let everyone pet him, and he licks the kids who come over to pet the doggie. "I'm Grateful Jake," he wags to them, "and I'm the luckiest dog in Savannah, don't you think?"

Daniel Watkins

208

CH. TRISKELION PRINCESS DESTINY CDX, CGC ("TRESA")

As far as Irish setters' lives go, I think I have it pretty good. I was born in Longmont, Colorado, and my canine parents are pretty impressive. My mom is a top-producing bitch, which means that she has made significant contributions to our breed in the production of champions in either the show ring, obedience, or in the field. My dad is a multiple best in show, multiple best in specialty show winner, and an American and Canadian champion. I am the oldest in my litter and was the first in my litter to win championship points, and I obtained my first obedience title of Companion Dog at eighteen months.

I have been all over the United States going to different kinds of dog shows. In 2000 I went to San Diego, California, and placed third in my class of over forty other girls. Later that same year, I got to go into the obedience ring for the first time in North Carolina, where I earned my Companion Dog title. It is also where I used to live before I moved to Savannah. Some of the other places I have been include Virginia, Indiana, Louisiana, Florida, New Jersey, New York City, and, of course, Georgia, where I live now.

In 2002 I qualified for the Westminster Kennel Club show held in New York City in February 2003. Shortly after that show, I continued my obedience career and obtained my Companion Dog Excellent title in the minimum amount of trials allowed. I guess I am pretty good at this obedience stuff because I got letters telling me that I am nationally ranked in the top ten obedience Irish setters for the year 2003 in both the Delaney and First and Foremost rankings. I was told that there are two different ranking systems, and sometimes a dog makes it into one or the other, but if they are really good at what they do, they make it into both systems at the same time. I was also ranked in the top-ten Irish setters that were shown at shows for all-breeds for the month of January 2003.

You would think that being this busy of a dog that I don't have time for my humans or for any fun. Nothing is further from the truth. I take my registered name of "Princess" very seriously. I might like to go play in the water sprinklers, but I sure don't like to get my feet wet in the rain or, for that matter, even go out in the rain. Now snow, that is a different subject. If it is deep enough, you can have all kinds of fun and maybe your humans will throw snowballs for you to catch in the air like mine did. Most of all, I like to counter surf and to snuggle on the couch with my humans.

TRESA

210

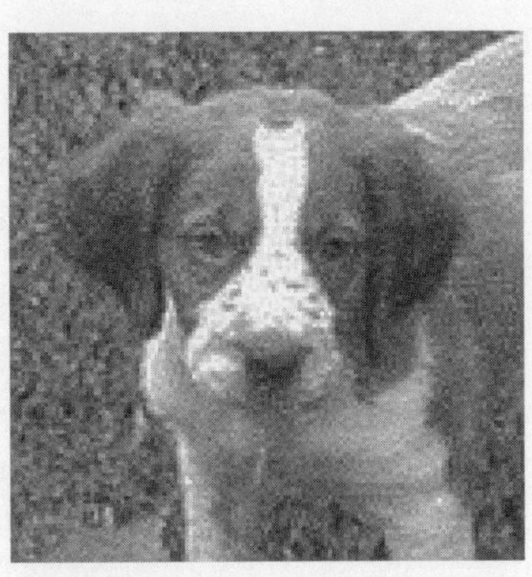

SPARKLE

The best names are frequently self-conferred. When my granddaughter Elizabeth was barely two, she announced, "I'm Biz!" And Biz she was, full of energy, buzzing around, and surprising everyone with intelligence far beyond her years and youthful appearance. The name just fit, and it stuck; she is still Biz, some twelve years later.

The self-conferring of appropriate names may be a rare thing, especially when the conferee has four feet and nine littermates. I knew after watching a new batch of ten Brittany puppies for several minutes that one of the females was a singular character. This little dog was joyous to watch: eager, curious, willing to join in a good tussle, and, although the largest male of the pack, was clearly the alpha—she was never far behind, and she was never daunted by the next new challenge. I was also aware that the finding of the right name for a dog was a serious matter, a task requiring insight into future performance and possible historic significance.

There are many references to the significant roles dogs have played throughout history. Everyone is familiar with the lines "The dog is man's best friend," "The little toy dog is cover with dust, but sturdy and stanch

211

he stands," "Every dog will have his day," and many more. Certainly there are a few that suggest dogs, like mankind, can have their ups and downs: "Lie down with dogs, get up with fleas," "going to the dogs," "Let sleeping dogs lie."

Obviously, naming this pup deserved careful thought. But almost at the same moment that I felt a sense of caution and care about selecting the best title for this young princess, the name "Sparkle" and then "Princess Sparkle" appeared for consideration, probably reserving the "Princess" for formal occasions.

There was, of course, one problem. I already knew a female of "singular character" who had previously acquired the highly appropriate nickname "Sparkle" and on occasion even merited the whole title, "Princess Sparkle." And this person was not only "alive and well," but worked in the office beside mine and had given me no reason to think that she might recognize that having a Brittany share her names and titles would be viewed as complimentary. So, I paused and considered alternatives, perhaps "Twinkle" being the best in a list of substitutes. But "Twinkle" and all the others simply did not fit. Both ladies had far too much strength of character, driving energy, and cool intelligence to be considered mere twinkles. In fact, "Twinkle" has associations that clearly lead in the wrong direction, toward images of Peter Pan and other childhood fantasies. Another clue may be found in the other nickname of "Sparkle 1st," which is "Kilowatt." No, "Twinkle" would never do.

After much thought, I simply asked the two "Sparkles" what they thought. Sparkle 2nd, the famous hunting dog to be, was gracious as I knew she would be. She knew she was "Sparkle" all the time. And "Sparkle 1st"? She is Karen Watts, RN, MSN, Director of

Outcomes and Performance Improvement at Memorial
Health, and one of the most intelligent, efficient, and
hard-working colleagues I have ever known. She was
thrilled.

FRANK E. CARLTON, M.D.

GETTY

My family tells me that if they believed in reincarnation they would hope to come back in their next life as Getty. That's my golden retriever. I guess they think that she is spoiled. I must admit that the old girl has it pretty good. She is an only child, and I say child because she thinks that she is human, which may be due to us treating her like one. Since we taught her to speak, she has been talking to us ever since, using a different tone for every particular demand. My favorite is one that we did not teach her. Every night she gets her belly rubbed while perched on the couch, where we said that we would never let her sit. If we stop too soon with the rubbing, she is quick to remind us with a low-growling moan. The longer we prolong the scratching, the louder she gets, along with wiggling just in case that we cannot hear her.

She has always been a dog with personality. While going through the routine on weekday mornings, she begins to pout. She will sulk on her bed, not even lifting her head when called. She will slightly cock her nose to the ceiling while slanting her eyes to reassure that she is ignoring any jester of consoling. Although this petty pout is heartbreaking, the returning-home greeting in the afternoon is well worth it. She will begin the sequence with a stretch leading to a wiggle. Her wagging tail becomes a full-body experience so much that her legs cannot hold her up. Then comes the howl-ing with excitement. Once all of these elements are com-bined, she collapses at my feet, belly-up with her upper lip flapped backwards to reveal a pearly white smile.

It is the little things that I appreciate about having Getty in my life. The generosity of her wanting to con-stantly share her squishy ball by laying it in my lap is never surprising. She is also willing to give up her time by taking us for evening walks, if she is not too stressed from guarding the homestead all day.

Getty does have a hobby, which is bird hunting. Her forte is the retrieving of doves for myself and sometimes for everyone else in the field as well. I guess that is her generosity shining through. Her favorite pastimes are terrorizing the ducks at the pond in our subdivision, smelling every blade of freshly cut grass, and gnawing every shred of thread from each of her toys.

Some people say that she is spoiled rotten. I think that she is loved.

HELEN HUSSEY

215

I came to my "mom" seven years ago on Christmas Eve. I remember the look of shock on her face when my "dad" gave me to her. You sse, I was a surprise. Even though Mom had been saying for years that she would like to have a daughter-dog, I think that she thought at that moment, "Be careful what you ask for."

Anyway, after the initial shock I could tell that Mom was as excited as the other family members who were present. The next thing on everyone's mind was that Mom should name me. Mom always had it in her mind that she would name her first dog "Pookie." When she was a little girl, she used to watch the "Soupy Sales Show." Soupy had two imaginary pets named Fang and Pookie. After watching that show many years ago, Mom made up her mind then that her baby dog would be "Pookie." Of course no one else in the family would hear of it. Comments included: "Pookie? You want to name her Angel or Snowflake or Noel since she is a Christmas gift." Finally Mom got so frustrated that she walked away. Dad found her and said, "What do *you* want to name him?" Mom said, "Pookie," and Dad said, "Pookie it is."

Fortunately everyone thinks that I have lived up to my name. You see, Mom pictured Pookie to be lovable, funny, and very active. I am all that and then some. I love my mom and dad, but not much of anyone else. I am *very* protective of my family and our house. I am very funny—funny ha-ha and funny strange. I am always making my parents laugh at my crazy antics, like when something comes over me and I have to run and run and run. Other times they think that it is funny and strange when I notice that Mom has changed shoes or a purse or put out a new decoration. I love to be active, especially outside. If I can't do that, I love to watch soap operas with Mom or sit on Dad's lap while he works on the computer. Mom and Dad tease me because they say that if I can't be with the one I love, I'll love the one I'm with.

All in all, we are all happy. Even though I'm an outdoor dog, I've managed to adjust to Mom and Dad's way of life. Mom finally got her daughter-dog, and even though Dad tries to act like he doesn't love me, I know he does. I think we make a good family.

On that fateful Christmas night seven years ago, the gift of the Pookie was a great thing for three people—well, two people and a dog.

POOKIE

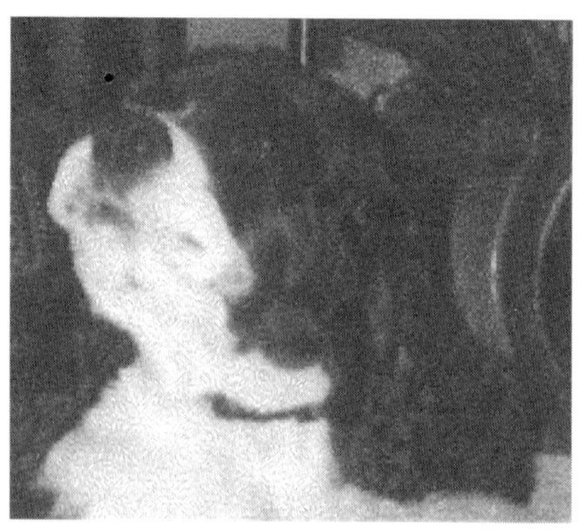

LUCILLE

Lucille and I met at a bookstore in Atlanta during Passover. I made a trip to the bookstore that beautiful, bright, spring afternoon because I was scheduled to teach a Sunday school lesson at my church the next day and I wanted to read more about this Jewish holiday that was occurring, and about which I was embarrassed to find I knew very little.

And there she was, sitting right by the door to the bookstore. I was unable to pass through the door of the store before her haunting black eyes caught my attention and my entire being. Those eyes spoke volumes, without one word passing between us. I, however, was a woman on a mission. I had to prepare for my Sunday school lesson, and I simply could not let those eyes stop me. We looked into each others' eyes for a few seconds, but I pushed the urge to talk to her down into my psyche and rushed headlong into the bookstore.

I spent a good deal of time in the religion section of the bookstore that day. After immersing myself in the theology found there in that huge, mega-dollar chain store, I finally made my purchases and strolled out the door to return home, feeling somehow enlightened and even happier because of my newfound religious mini-education. To my amazed delight, those black eyes were still there outside the store, and in my enlightened state I decided to stop for a short chat.

Lucille, it turns out, was a homeless and abused black-and-white spaniel of some kind. She was so small and her paws were so large that she looked just like a puppy. I chatted with her through the panels of the large pen that held her and about five other small dogs. It only took about three seconds for us to bond, and I knew within that time that I could not walk away from that poor little puppy. Yet, reality has a cold way of creeping into warm, fuzzy situations. I rationalized: I lived alone in a townhouse apartment in the middle of a huge city, with no fenced-in yard, and not even any grass to speak of even remotely near to my front door. I worked at a job where I put in long hours. How could I even consider adopting a homeless dog, much less one that seemed to have been abused and probably therefore had "issues" that would need to be met and overcome?

I returned to my car with the heaviest heart I'd felt in a long time. There was no way. A dog simply could not fit into my life at that time. I sat down in the driver's seat and wept. I wept for the little dog that had just been passed over, but it was not a Passover that would have allowed her to be saved. That little black-eyed dog may have just received a death sentence because of her passover. And I wept for myself because I had also somehow allowed myself to be passed by simply walking away from her.

I thought of how the Passover is the celebration that reminds us of how the Lord saved and protected the Israelites during a time of bondage and slavery. I thought of how there really are no coincidences in our lives, because God carefully and lovingly puts things in our paths at times that might save and protect us from the bondage and slavery of our own lives. Maybe a dog was just what I needed to prevent me from spending long, lonely hours at an office and job that was getting me nowhere.

I raced back to the store. Yes, I would adopt the little black-and-white dog with those piercing black eyes. I found out that her name was Lucille; that little was known of her except that she had been adopted and returned by at least two families. Returned? It was difficult to imagine that anyone could have given up that little bundle of curly fur.

We drove home with a car filled with a pet carrier, leashes, treats, and of course the forgotten books. Those books have been placed on a shelf, or maybe in a long-forgotten box, but the Passover lesson so carefully unveiled to me by an unseen hand that day still lives with me. We spent fourteen dog years (two human years) living in Atlanta, but in 2003 we moved to Savannah, where I rnarried my best friend and soul mate, Lawrence B. Lee. Lucille took a little while to adjust to having Larry in her life, but she still thinks that she is the love of my life, and I don't tell her anything different.

That little dog is a daily, joyful reminder of the beauty that can come in small packages. It is nearly impossible to describe the happiness that comes from that little dog, who will always look like a puppy, and who greets me every time I return from even the shortest trip as if I had been gone forever, and as if she never thought she would see me again. That kind of joy can only be infectious in the most positive way to any human life that is touched.

Kristin Tolvstad Lee

MIRACLE

The evening that I found and brought home Miracle was just another end of a day, or at least I thought it was.

A short trip to the pharmacy at Victory Drive and Skidaway Road started a now almost twelve-year journey.

When I drove up to the pharmacy, I noticed a few people standing next to the old Miracle Ear. They were surrounding a small dog. I proceeded into the pharmacy knowing that when I left the store I would need to find out more.

Almost not wanting to get involved with another dog rescue, I did. I had no choice. Call it divine intervention or just a plain miracle, but I had to check out what the fuss was about.

Upon gazing at the scared, pregnant, desperate creature, I knew immediately I would help. The dog had made her way safely to the outside of the building and decided she could go no further. According to the other people that evening, she had been there the biggest part of the day. They had contacted Animal Control and decided not to pursue the animal control pickup for fear she would be put down.

The darkness of the evening was quickly approaching, and as the other individuals at the scene soon surmised, I was there for the rescue. With their minds at ease the crowd dispersed.

I summoned my partner on the telephone with a statement that went something like this: "There's a dog up here that needs help and she's been here all day, can you please come help me with her?" Although I knew that I was about to hear the same reply I have heard from her many times regarding helpless and stray animals, she reluctantly and not so enthusiastically said, "Okay!" The find, the rescue, and the help came very naturally. The ability to carry out the complete pickup and responsibility for caring, nurturing, and vet visits has been shared by both of us.

My partner Heather arrived immediately to help. Actually she did all the work. I simply coached, encouraged, supported, and opened the car door for her to lift the pregnant, scared animal into my car. So to speak, the thrill of the find and rescue is quickly followed by, "Now what are we going to do?"

We took her home and tried to make her feel as comfortable as we could. After all, she had lain there next to the Miracle Ear and Revco all day waiting for her new life to begin. Not only was *her* new life about to begin, but also those of five of the sweetest puppies that have ever been born. Heather took Miracle—the new name was so appropriate—to the vet the following day. She came home that evening with a video and instructions on how to help a dog deliver. Two days passed, then, on Wednesday, October 29, 1992, our Miracle gave birth to Bootsie, Summerville, Squeeky, Bandit, and Spanky, two boys and three girls. What an experience—one that I know Heather and I will never forget.

The journey through the years that have followed has been like a TV sitcom that could have been called "The Kids: Tails from Talahi Island."

The beginning with the mother, Miracle, and her five puppies was great. She was a great mom. The puppies quickly grew, and oh how we loved them all.

We knew though, we would need to try and find homes for them. It was so very hard.

Summerville, one of the males, had been named after a friend here in Savannah that we were hoping would take her. Not so, but oddly enough he was adopted by a family in Sommerville, South Carolina, that renamed him Beethoven. He continues to live happily ever after with his family and a pot-bellied pig.

Spanky, one of the females, was adopted for two days by a couple on the Southside of Savannah. They called back to say that she did not fit into their home with their other animals. We could not get there fast enough to bring her back home. Spanky's been with us ever since.

Bandit, a female, was adopted by a couple in Richmond Hill. He was a military man and they had two young kids. They lived in a very nice house with a swimming pool and creek in the backyard. How do I know this? From time to time I checked on her peering through the fence. It was one of the last times that I checked on her that a neighbor approached me and said, "May I help you?" I explained to him that I had given Bandit to them a couple of years ago and that I was just looking in on her.

He told me that the man had been shipped overseas and that the wife was having a difficult time with all of her responsibilities. He thought that she was probably going to find Bandit a new home. I gave him my business card and told him that I would help if she needed it. Well, it wasn't a week later that she called. Once again, we could not drive there fast enough to retrieve our Bandit and bring her home.

After all, we still had Miracle, Bootsie, Spanky, and Squeeky. After giving away Summerville and Bandit, the separation had proved to be so dramatic that we did not even try to find Bootsie or Squeeky a new family. They never left home. Once again, with the exception of Summerville, the kids were back together.

We were together again for another nine or so years before Bandit passed away. Our hearts were broken.

The Miracle that happened to us almost twelve years ago was one of unity, love, and family. Our Miracle is now in her golden years, and Bootsie, Squeeky, and Spanky are living happily with us on Talahi.

SUSAN SPEROS

NEFERTITTEE
("TITTEE")

Tittee was born on February 13, 2004, in a litter of three miniature Doberman puppies. Her father is Sebastian and her mother is Cleopatra. Two of the puppies died soon after birth, and the mother refused to feed Tittee. We fed her around the clock with a bottle, and, lo and behold, she survived.

She is very active and loves playing with all her friends. Lucky and Shelbe are bulldogs, Fancee Laddee is a cocker spaniel, and Sebastian is a miniature Doberman.

I love to take Tittee to the dog carnivals and dress her up in all kinds of costumes. She loves it. At the last carnival everybody laughed because Tittee entered the biscuit-eating contest and only weighed two pounds. Big mistake—she won.

What I love most about my Nefertittee is when it is time for bed and we curl up together and go to sleep. I say a prayer of thanks that my Tittee survived, because she is my precious gift from above.

KATIE JUNE SAUNDERS

How Loyal Are Dogs?

How loyal are dogs? By that, I mean if a dog and its master were in a deep-trouble situation, would the dog run or stay behind and help the master? We know the answer to that one, I think. Too many instances of dogs protecting their masters to indicate otherwise.

But how loyal are dogs to one another? I don't know the full answer, but let me tell you a story that shows true loyalty. Not only by one dog, but by three. This happened a long time ago—at least seventy years.

Frank Free was my uncle. Actually, an uncle-by-marriage because his wife, Leone, was my mother's sister. They lived at Millhaven, Georgia, on a sixteen thousand–acre farm owned by Mrs. E. T. Comer of Savannah. My uncle was the rural mail carrier for Millhaven and vicinity. His daily route ran sixty miles, and to me that was an excellent occupation. Indeed, he was home by 2 P.M., and after dinner (lunch was called dinner in those days) he could hunt, fish, play baseball, or do anything else that struck his fancy.

During the Great Depression, when Dad was laid off by the Georgia Railroad in Augusta, I was lodged with Frank and Leone for the three years it took for Dad to get back on his feet and to become a marine engineer.

Uncle Frank had three dogs—Judge and Lady, pointers, and Sport, a setter. One day he brought home another setter, Joe, who was the most mange-eaten animal I'd ever seen. Who gave him that dog I cannot remember, but I well remember Frank and Leone's attention to Joe, giving him medicine, on the outside and inside, to cure that mange. The other three dogs immediately took to Joe, and were as attentive as the rest of us while Joe's mange was cured and he became as handsome as the others.

Joe also was a good hunter, as the other dogs were, and as a child of ten or eleven I always enjoyed going hunting with my uncle and watching the dogs retrieve the birds my uncle shot. Never did a dog do anything but what he was expected to do, and the dogs were like one happy family.

But one day that changed. Joe was in the road, in front of the Frees' home, when along came a speeding car and struck Joe before he could get out of the way. Bam! Aunt Leone and I, inside the house, could hear that awful crash, and we both ran to the front to see that it was. The car had stopped, and Joe lay dead just behind it. I mean dead. He was as still as anything I'd ever seen.

The driver of the car was very upset. He swore he didn't see the dog, and he joined my aunt and me in a good cry. I doubt that he ever got over it, and we never did. We knew the driver, and he knew the story of Joe's recovery from his attack of mange.

An hour or so later, Frank drove home from his mail route, and he too had a good cry over Joe. He got a shovel, dug a hole in the backyard, and buried the dog, while the other three dogs looked on as their good friend was lowered into the grave and covered with dirt.

Frank came in and we ate dinner, and darned if I ever could remember what we had. It was a sad day, indeed.

Then came the night, and as soon as darkness had set in we could hear something we had never quite heard before. Howling we had heard, but this howling was different. Very different. We walked to the front porch and looked out. There, in the middle of the road where Joe had met his demise, Judge, Lady, and Sport kept howling.

And I kid you not—they howled, over and over again, "Joeeee . . . Joeeee . . . Joeeee" . . . on and on. They howled nearly all night. And for three nights in succession.

That, to my uncle, aunt, and me, was loyalty. Deep, abiding loyalty. To a dear friend—Joe!

And this story comes from someone who, himself, never owned a dog.

TOM COFFEY